THE OUTLAW'S JOURNEY

A mythological approach to storytelling for writers behind bars

by

Gloria Kempton

To Janette, Be the Hero of your Journey! Gloria Kempton

Foreword by Christopher Vogler

Introduction © 2013 Christopher Vogler

Book & cover designed by Vladimir Verano, Third Place Press

Cover imagery: © miklas1; mycola; abzee-via iStockphoto.com

ISBN: 978-1-60944-072-5

Outlaw's Journey

4701 SW Admiral Way
#407
Seattle, WA 98116
Email: outlawsjourney@gmail.com

Printed at Third Place Press, Lake Forest Park, WA on the Espresso Book Machine v.2.2.
www.thirdplacepress.com

TABLE OF CONTENTS

FOREWORD

WELCOME TO THE ADVENTURE OF WRITING. If you've decided to give it a whirl by following the steps in this course, I can promise you many hours of enjoyable mental activity. You'll be expressing yourself and having the satisfaction of finishing a writing project, but more importantly you'll discover things about yourself that you never imagined possible. By putting your stories down on paper, you'll be taking a journey into your mind and spirit, no matter where your body happens to be. And on that journey, you will be automatically, effortlessly, reviewing your own life and putting it into a healthier perspective.

This course of step-by-step instructions for writing a story is inspired, in part, by a book I wrote called *The Writer's Journey: Mythic Structure for Writers*. You'll read many times in this course about ideas I described in that book. The main idea is something called *The Hero's Journey* which is a pattern of story-telling that's as old as time, and yet it's something that the most modern and experimental of film-makers and novelists use every day.

It's the old story from myths and fairy tales. Somebody sets out from home into a new world of thrills and danger. There he or she gets tangled up in a life and death struggle between powerful forces, some benign and helpful, some hostile and threatening. The traveler is severely challenged by this struggle, facing his or her greatest fear, and maybe even goes to the point of death before being transformed by the experience into something new -- a hero -- who has transcended the boundaries of life and death. Then, despite further challenges, our hero brings home some treasure won on the adventure, and a new understanding of what is possible.

Sound familiar? It should. It's the spine of almost every good movie or novel, and it's an accurate picture of what we all go through at different passages in our lives.

In *The Writer's Journey* I broke that story down into twelve stages that described what I found in my own life, in the stories and movies I loved as a kid, and in the Hollywood movies I was working on in my career. (I spent most of my life reading scripts and writing reports on them for the Hollywood studios.) In creating my twelve-step outline of story-telling, I was inspired by the work of a man named Joseph Campbell, an American philosopher and scholar of mythology whose most important book is *The Hero with a Thousand Faces*. He was a big influence on novelists and film-makers, such as George Lucas who has said he could never have created the Star Wars saga without Campbell's ideas.

I found Campbell's work when I was a film student, and I can say quite honestly it changed my life. First, it gave me an edge in the competitive world of Hollywood; now I knew the secret keys to storytelling. But much more important, it opened up a way of thinking about life. I realized *The Hero's Journey* was a good blueprint for telling stories, but it also turned out to be a great set of guidelines for how to get through almost any challenging experience.

I adapted Campbell's ideas and terms to reflect what I saw in modern movies, and, after a challenging Hero's Journey of my own, finally found a publisher and launched my first book, *The Writer's Journey*. Over the years I was happy to see that it was accepted as a textbook in many college writing classes and that serious screenwriters and novelists were using it to help structure their stories and improve their dramatic impact. But I also had the sneaking suspicion that it could be much, much more.

And over the years as I went around conducting writing workshops, people would come up to me, sometimes with great emotion, to say how the ideas in the book had changed their lives, or how they had found unexpected ways to use the pattern in arenas that had nothing to do with writing a story or making a movie. It turned out, as I had expected, that *The Hero's Journey* pattern has uses in areas as far-flung as planning a trip, launching a new product, re-organizing a business, staging a wedding, designing a scientific experiment, producing a PowerPoint slideshow, choreographing a dance, composing a rap song, surviving a life-threatening illness, making sense of a divorce or a tragic death, or, surprise, surprise, helping prisoners make sense of their lives through telling their own stories.

That's why I'm happy to introduce this new course for writers who happen to be in prison somewhere. Your mentor and guide for this adventure in storytelling and self-discovery, Gloria Kempton, has adapted *The Hero's Journey* ideas into a step-by-step, easy to follow set of lessons that will give you everything you need to tell the story that's waiting inside you. There's a lot of useful information here, because Gloria has not only made a clear explanation of *The Hero's Journey* outline but she has also provided you with all the other little bits and pieces you will need to make your story shine. There's solid, wise advice about dialogue, character, genre, pacing, subtext, and many other writing tricks of the trade. It's all given in bite-sized pieces so you can take them one at a time and it won't seem overwhelming. If you just follow along and do the writing exercises as she suggests, you'll soon have a complete story you can be proud of.

Don't think of the exercises as work, but as a kind of play, like letting a strong, powerful horse out of the barn for a trot across the countryside.

Part of *The Hero's Journey* that you'll encounter in this course is an idea called "archetypes" which is the notion that there are certain simple character types that you can find over and over again in stories, such as the hero, the shadow or villain who opposes him, the herald who warns him, the mentor who guides him, the trickster who tries to outwit him, the threshold guardian who blocks his progress on the path, the shapeshifter who confuses him with changing appearances, and the ally who supports him. Gloria has made an original contribution to the growing field of Hero's Journey studies, by drawing attention to another archetype, the outlaw.

It's a romantic word with strong associations from the American West and the world of gunslingers, bandits and cattle rustlers, but it has its roots in a much older world, that of the Vikings. In olden times in Iceland, Vikings were lusty and violent, but sometimes even they needed to isolate certain people who were just too dangerous to society. They called them "outlaws" because they were officially outside the protection of the law, and anyone was free to mistreat them or even kill them without fear of punishment. But though they were a menace to society, sometimes good things came from outlaws. Good things like the discovery of America.

The most famous Viking outlaw was a fellow named Eric the Red, the son of a hot-head who was banished from Viking society in Norway for his violent ways. Eric's father took his family to the distant island colony of Iceland, a wild and dangerous place, but there Eric was too violent for the locals and so they made him an outlaw, too, and he was forced to set sail for unknown lands. The Icelanders expected him to just sail off the map and die, but instead he discovered Greenland and founded a colony there that lasted for hundreds of years, long before Columbus. Outlaws stand at the edge of society, and from there they can sometimes see visions of unknown countries that ordinary people never glimpse.

Gloria is a good and trustworthy guide to the new country you're about to explore. Trust her guidance and the writing instincts in your gut. In *The Writer's Journey* I conclude with a chapter where I talk about a moment in my life where I'd screwed up everything royally, and on my own Hero's Journey had to come almost to the point of death before I realized an important lesson, which is "Trust the Path." That means trust your own instincts and trust the process of writing, which is something much older than you. You are walking an ancient trail, the path of the storyteller. By choosing to tell your story, you're part of something, the long parade of storytellers through the ages. You'll have doubts and setbacks — that's part of the journey -- but in the end you'll look back on your writing journey with satisfaction. Trust the story within you. The story knows the way.

Good luck, and enjoy the adventure.

Chris Vogler
Author of *The Writer's Journey*

ACKNOWLEDGMENTS

A BIG THUMBS UP TO CHRISTOPHER VOGLER for writing *The Writer's Journey;* you have made Joseph Campbell's *The Hero's Journey* accessible to thousands and thousands of new writers and seasoned writers alike. Your approach offers a way to make meaning out of the stories we write that reflect both the pain and joy of the human experience. I'll be forever grateful for the day I picked up *The Writer's Journey* and was introduced in such a powerful way to my own life through the stories I was writing then and the ones I'm writing now.

Kudos to the man himself, Joseph Campbell. I never had the opportunity to meet you until you were gone, but your work has informed my life in so many ways and continues to do so every day as I learn more and more about who I am as the hero of the journey that is my life.

Finally, to the men in our Twin Rivers and Washington State Reformatory *Hero's Journey* writing groups. You inspire me every single day as I think about you waking up each morning and choosing to live your Hero's Journey with such meaning, purpose and integrity in a difficult situation. You are the inspiration for this course and the true heroes in my world.

HOW TO USE THIS BOOK

THIS COURSE IS INTENDED FOR WRITERS who are currently behind bars, but there may be some of you reading this book who simply want to take the course to learn how to write stories that incorporate *The Hero's Journey*, or maybe just to learn the writing craft and receive feedback on your writing. We welcome you.

Following are just a few things we want you to know and a few requests:

- This book is designed to be used as a correspondence course where you turn in lessons and receive feedback from a professional writing instructor who, by the way, is first and foremost a writer like yourself. However, if, for whatever reason, you don't want to take the course at this time, you can get a good handle on both *The Hero's Journey* and the writing craft just by reading this book.

- There are twelve stages of *The Hero's Journey*, and so we expect you to complete the course within one year—one chapter per month. If you get behind, for a small fee ($50), you can request an extension.

- You may have a story in mind to work on during the course, but if you simply want to use the course for the purpose of exercising your writing muscles, that's fine, too. And you can change tracks midway and work on a different story than the one you started with, but you have to keep going from where you left off, rather than starting the course over with a different story.

• We prefer that you type your assignments, but if you don't have access to a typewriter or computer, we will accept handwritten work, as long as you print legibly.

• Please make sure you honor the word limits for each lesson; if you exceed them, we'll ask you to cut before we review your work.

• We promise to turn your work around as quickly as we can, but we need at least two, sometimes three, weeks to get your assignments back to you.

• We can only look at assignments one time; no revisions of previous assignments, please.

• Please send us a photo of yourself, if you have one. It's nice to be able to put a face with the words on the page.

• Please include a self-addressed stamped envelope with each assignment you submit to us for the return of your next assignment.

• At the end of the course, if you complete all of the assignments, we'll send you a Certificate of Completion.

• The price of the course is $595 and must be paid for in full at the time of enrollment. Please send your check to the address below. (Contact us if you need to make other arrangements for payment.)

• When you sign up for the correspondence course, the book is free.

• We understand that as a writer behind bars, you may need financial help in order to enroll in this course. Feel free to contact us about scholarship opportunities.

• Contact info for your assignments or any other correspondence:

The Outlaw's Journey

4701 SW Admiral Way

#407

Seattle, WA 98116

Email: outlawsjourney@gmail.com

PERSONAL PROFILE

THE QUESTIONS BELOW are designed to help us get to know you and so that you might begin to consider which of the many stories you have in your head that you might like to write. Please answer the questions in as much detail as you'd like and send them to us with your first assignment.

1. What is your full name? And what is the name you'd like us to use when addressing you in our reviews of your work?

2. How long have you been in prison? How much more time do you have to serve?

3. Can you give us a brief history of your writing background? (When you started writing, what you like to write, if you've ever been published, etc.)

4. What kind of stories do you most like to read? Novels, memoirs, short stories, personal experience stories? Genre (action/adventure, horror, literary, mainstream, sci-fi, fantasy, romance, suspense thriller, mystery)? List your five favorite authors and/or novels/memoirs.

5. Are you familiar with Joseph Campbell and/or *The Hero's Journey*? What are the one or two most important things you'd like to discover about your writing self or accomplish with your writing by the end of *The Outlaw's Journey* course?

6. How strongly do you feel about getting your work published? Is this a goal?

7. Anything else you'd like us to know (where you're from, marital status, kids, hobbies, writing dreams)?

THE OUTLAW'S JOURNEY

INTRODUCTION

"SO IN *THE HERO'S JOURNEY*, THERE'S THE *ORDINARY WORLD*, which is your personal or your character's everyday life, then there's the *Special World*, which is the world of the story." I sat back to look around the room at the group of men, satisfied with my explanation so far of this complicated storytelling system that is both our real lives and the lives of our fictional characters.

Gabriel looked at me, a surprised, quizzical and appalled look on his face. "So prison is the '*Special*' World'?" *How could this be?* his expression said. *I'm supposed to see prison as my "special" world? What are you smoking, anyway?*

Okay, so it's not like we're always delighted with the *Hero's Journey* we've been given. We don't even always choose it. Sometimes we just find ourselves there, like Dorothy in *The Wizard of Oz*. She gets hit on the head during a storm and wakes up in Oz.

In some way you may have been tossed into a storm and hit on the head, too, metaphorically speaking, and awakened in prison, now on a journey not of your choosing. Or at least you didn't consciously choose it. Your soul may have chosen it for you.

You've committed a crime (or possibly innocent but have been accused of a crime) and now you live in a 6 x 8 foot cell. You're watched 24 hours per day. You seldom get one moment to yourself to think a thought, take a leak, make a private phone call. You have little control over anything at all in your life, and it may be this way for a while. You've hurt someone and because you're paying the consequences, you're reminded of what you did every single day. Much of society has written you off, and depending on the kind of crime you've committed, does not want to see you out on the streets again any time soon, if ever. This is because, in society's perception, you're a drug dealer, a bank robber, a murderer, a burglar—in short, an outlaw. You've taken a path that is literally outside of the law, and society has a way of dealing with those who do that.

And yet, even though you're only too aware of all of the above, something else is also true. You're a hero. There is indeed someone in charge of your life and that someone is you. You're the hero of your life, hereafter called your journey. Oh, society wouldn't call you a hero. They think of a hero as the dictionary defines it: Somebody who commits an act of great courage, strength of character, or another admirable quality, somebody who is admired and looked up to for outstanding qualities or achievements. If your life were a story, and it is, society might look at you and stamp you with one label. Villain. Criminal. Outlaw. Certainly not hero.

But society doesn't get the last say. Your life is a story, and you're the main character. And it does take a lot of courage and strength of character to live the life you've chosen, one that sent you to prison. So, for the sake of our purposes in this writing course, the definition of a hero is simply how Wikipedia (the most used online resource for quickly defining a word) would define it: *a character, who, in the face of danger and adversity or from a position of weakness, displays courage and the will for self-sacrifice—that is, heroism—for some greater good of all humanity. This definition originally referred to martial courage or excellence but extended to more general moral excellence.* (See Lesson Three for an expanded definition of the hero archetype.)

Now, it's up to you to see yourself that way, or if writing a fictional story, to portray your character in that light, as displaying courage from a position of weakness. As a prisoner, you're in an *external* position of weakness (repeat—*external*--wouldn't want you to see it any other way as I'm fully aware of what happens to *weak* men in prison), whether you see it that way or not. At the same time, you have to believe that, on some level, you have the kind of moral excellence of a true hero who is, though not necessarily on a conscious level, in exile.

This is what *The Hero's Journey* is all about—you on an external journey to prison—not your conscious choice—for a period of self-imposed exile in order to explore the inner landscape of your human journey.

You may wonder if *The Hero's Journey* is about religion; it's not, though you can be a religious person and explore the inner landscape of your personal journey with the Bible or any other religious book by your side. The hero in *The Hero's Journey* is an explorer. While your external world is closed off to you at the moment, maybe for many years, this is your opportunity to explore the inner landscape of yourself as a human being. Just because you're in prison, your journey isn't over. It may be just beginning. It all depends on how much exploring of your inner landscape you've done before becoming incarcerated.

As a young writer, story structure was a mystery to me for many years. Then, upon the recommendation of a writer friend I trusted, I picked up Christopher Vogler's *The Writer's Journey* and started reading. I may have gotten as far as the second stage, *The Call to Adventure,* and felt completely lost. I didn't pick the book up again until about eight years later. That time I was ready, and the archetypes, the stages of the journey—I could see it all in my own life. I recognized *The Hero's Journey* because it was my life story.

It's also your life story. This is what *The Hero's Journey is*—a system, a way of thinking about our lives, a way to shape and revise and rewrite our personal life stories. Whether we use the form of memoir or novel, personal experience story or short story.

If you want to get the most out of this course, I would recommend that you have someone send you a copy of Christopher Vogler's book, *The Writer's Journey.* You could also dig into Joseph Campbell's *The Hero with a Thousand Faces,* but because Campbell is more challenging to "get" than Vogler, *The Writer's Journey* is a better choice for this course.

WHAT IS *THE HERO'S JOURNEY?*

I HAVE A PIECE OF ART ON MY BEDROOM WALL. Underneath the painting, the caption reads: *"Anyone can slay a dragon. Try waking up in the morning and loving the world all over again; that's what takes a real hero."*

The Hero's Journey is ultimately the path of love. It is a powerful metaphor for the agony and the ecstasy of our human lives on this planet. Chris Vogler writes in *The Writer's Journey: The Hero's Journey is not an invention, but an observation. It is a recognition of a beautiful design, a set of principles that govern the conduct of life and the world of storytelling the way physics and chemistry govern the physical world...The Hero's Journey is a pattern that seems to extend in many dimensions, describing more than one reality. It accurately describes, among other things, the process of making a journey, the necessary working parts of a story, the joys and despairs of being a writer, and the passage of a soul through life.*

- *The process of making a journey*

  According to The Hero's Journey, we move through certain stages in our lives as we pursue our goals and dreams. We confront our demons, slay dragons, emerge as heroes. Or not. (We will explore the not—the tragic hero--in our third lecture.)

- *The necessary working parts of a story*

  A story is the development of one specific conflict in a person's or character's life. The Hero's Journey is a way of ordering that conflict, shaping it so as to make meaning out of it.

- *The joys and despairs of being a writer*

  Our stories are not easily shaped as it takes deep, and often painful, exploration and inquiry in which only a select few writers are willing to engage. Fortunately, the process of this kind of deep storytelling also has its own rewards.

- *The passage of a soul through life*

  The Hero's Journey captures and holds the external movement of a life and discovers and interprets the internal themes in an intimate relationship between writer and reader.

HOW DOES THE HERO'S JOURNEY INFORM OUR LIVES AND OUR WRITING?

AT FIRST GLANCE, *THE HERO'S JOURNEY* might seem like a formula for plotting our stories and/or interpreting our lives, but it's far from it. For one thing, a life isn't so neatly ordered in 12 stages, although if you know *The Hero's Journey*, and you look closely, you will find them all there as the person navigates the situation, whatever it is. They may not occur in the exact order as *The Hero's Journey* dictates, but if it's a true *Hero's Journey*, they're there. The archetypes are there, too, the players in the story sometimes shifting from one to another, but again, if you know the archetypes, and you look closely, you can identify each one of them. Because this is what a *Hero's Journey is*. It's an adventure, and what makes it an adventure is that we didn't plan it, and it's bigger than we are. An adventure, according to the dictionary, is an undertaking involving uncertainty and risk—definitely a *Hero's Journey*.

Why *The Hero's Journey*, though? Why not just grab a how-to-plot or how-to-write-a-memoir book or take a writing class, if your prison offers one? Many writers do just that. They learn by trial and error. As I mentioned above, I did that myself for many years. I bumbled along writing my little stories that ended up conveying even littler themes, if I could find the theme at all. Most of the time, I just tacked one on. As a writing coach, I see many of the writers I work with do this. But *The Hero's Journey* is a powerful tool for helping us dig out the deeper and more important themes of our stories. Once we know how to use it, we can begin to explore the deeper meanings in our stories, the universal truths that are there inherent in our stories if we know what to look for and where to look for it.

The Hero's Journey does other things, too, all of which we'll discuss in the lessons that follow. It begins to show us our attitude toward our lives and stories, our resistance to some of the lessons we could be learning, and our shadow that is hiding the story truths we're not quite ready to look at. *The Hero's Journey* is a giant flashlight that can be used to illuminate the stories that burn passionately in our hearts, and when we're ready to write them, it's there, waiting to help us make meaning out of those stories.

WHAT IS THE CRITERIA FOR A *HERO'S JOURNEY* STORY?

NOT EVERY STORY IS A *HERO'S JOURNEY*. The writer's recognition of the lessons and meaning inherent in a personal experience or in a character's dramatic conflict in a novel is what makes the story a journey. A personal essay is not a *Hero's Journey*, though it can have some of the elements, as you discover that, say, another person in your life is wearing the mask of the "threshold guardian" and trying to prevent you from accomplishing a dream. Or that you received a "call to adventure," when your boss wore the mask of the "herald," and told you he was laying you off. To write a personal essay is to explore a topic, but the form doesn't allow you to order your exploration so neatly as to put it into stages as a story does (whether real or fictional). Many plot-driven genre stories are not hero's journeys in that they stay on the surface of the protagonist's experience. A genre story *can* be a *Hero's Journey* if the writer chooses to take the protagonist deeper than the surface. In short, what makes a story a *Hero's Journey* is the writer's ability to perceive the meaning in the hero's experience, not always something that's immediately evident, especially if the hero is the writer himself.

A *Hero's Journey* includes at least the following five elements: 1) a main character who is about something bigger than just saving his own skin,

2) an external and internal dramatic conflict, 3) the recognition of the archetypes that play specific roles in the story, 4) a theme that is universal, and 5) a writer who is willing to mine the story for the depths of the stages of the journey, the archetypes, and his or her own life. We will be discussing all of the criteria in more depth in the following lessons, so we hope you'll hang on for the ride and learn how to recognize your own life's *Hero's Journey* and those of your characters'.

Who came up with this idea of *The Hero's Journey*, anyway? A man named Joseph Campbell, an American mythologist, who wanted to explore the theory that important myths from around the world which have survived for thousands of years all share a fundamental structure, which Campbell called the monomyth. In a well-known quote from the introduction to *The Hero with a Thousand Faces*, Campbell summarized the monomyth:

A hero ventures forth from the world of common day into a region of supernatural wonder: fabulous forces are there encountered and a decisive victory is won: the hero comes back from this mysterious adventure with the power to bestow boons on his fellow man. (Wikipedia: *The Hero with a Thousand Faces*)

The only criteria that's required of you as the hero of your journey is that you have a sincere desire to authenticate, explore, and reflect on your human journey thus far and be open to whatever you discover is up ahead for you as you outline your story during the next few weeks or months.

THE STAGES

The Hero's Journey has 12 stages and 8 archetypes. These are what we'll be studying during the next few weeks and months, with an added ninth archetype—the outlaw. Following is a short summary for your reference.

The protagonist/hero goes through various stages on his journey, beginning in his *Ordinary World* and then finally arriving "home" on his *Return with the Elixir*. These stages can be external and/or internal, and the most effective stories incorporate both the external and the internal. These stages are meant to test the hero, to severely challenge him so that, whether you're writing a short story, novel, or literary memoir, by the end of the story, the protagonist is a different person than when he started out. Following is a brief description of each stage of the journey:

The Ordinary World – The context, home base and background of the hero, the home turf, the hood; something, someone, some event rocks the hero's perception of himself, his world, and those populating this world; hero is poised to break free from this world, ready to enter the world of adventure.

Call to Adventure – Herald announces the journey, the stakes of the game; makes clear the hero's goal--to achieve the dream, survive the journey, confront the challenge, transcend the ego, transform a life; often a moment where the hero simply runs out of options.

Refusal of the Call – Fear, terror of the unknown; not yet fully committed to the journey, still thinking of turning back; makes effort to dodge the adventure; forced to examine the quest carefully and redefine its objectives; makes excuses; persistent refusal creates a tragic hero; conflicting calls; *Ordinary World* calls to hero to turn back; appearance of threshold guardians.

Meeting with the Mentor – Greek word, *menos*, meaning intention, force or purpose--mind, spirit or remembrance; mentor's role is to prepare the hero to meet the unknown; may offer advice, guidance, magical equipment; appears at the hero's moments of doubt; energy of mentor may show up embodied as a person, tradition, or code of ethics; mentors are enthused about learning, pass that enthusiasm on to hero.

Crossing the First Threshold – Overcoming fear; decision to commit to the journey/adventure; a zone of crossing that may be desolate and lonely or crowded with life; feeling the loss of the familiar; encounters more threshold guardians.

Tests, Allies, Enemies – Enters the new unexplored and emotional territory of the special world; test to prepare for the rest of the journey; appearance of allies and enemies; begins to sort friends and enemies--who can be trusted and who can't; may encounter the shadow and face threatening events; often teams are formed.

Approach to the Inmost Cave – Prepares for the ordeal to come; possesses a degree of confidence because of already-passed tests; faces down enemies; becomes aware of the ticking clock; faces higher stakes if refusing to proceed; takes inventory; gets into opponent's mind, breakthrough.

The Ordeal – Life or death moment—can be external, internal, or both; directly confronts greatest fear; crisis of the heart, death of the ego; comes away forever changed; moves from focus on self to focus on group; wins right to be called "hero."

Reward – Seizes the sword--tangible or internal, takes possession; new perceptions; sees through deception (moment of clarity); self-realization, epiphany.

The Road Back – Decision to return to the *Ordinary World* and implement lessons learned; faces skeptics and doubters; lure of the past rises up; former demons appear once again; time for hero to watch his back; elation after enduring ordeal; back in reality, hero's resolve called into question.

The Resurrection – Showdown; final exam to see if lessons are really learned; not a time to relax; faces choice—to follow violent code of the *Ordinary World* or the peaceful way learned in the special world; purification before return to community, cleansing; hero acts rather than lets himself be rescued; sacrifice—something must be surrendered (old habit or belief); climax and catharsis in mind, body, and emotion; point where greatest awareness is reached; incorporation of lessons; proof of inner change and lessons learned; transformation.

Return with the Elixir – Magic potion with the power to heal, sometimes so powerful that it brings about change in everyone around the hero; might be love, wisdom, responsibility; sometimes sadder but wiser; punctuation at the end of the sentence (period, exclamation point, question mark, ellipses).

(Adapted from *The Writer's Journey* by Chris Vogler)

THE ARCHETYPES

AN ARCHETYPE, IN PSYCHOLOGY, IS A MODEL (a type) of a person, personality, or behavior. Carl G. Jung is the one who first coined the word to suggest "the existence of universal contentless forms that channel experiences and emotions, resulting in recognizable and typical patterns of behavior with certain probable outcomes." (Wikipedia) For storytellers using *The Hero's Journey*, an archetype is a certain type of character. The storyteller isn't inventing characters at random just to populate the story--each character has a role to play. Each character in your cast of characters has an archetype and so, a purpose. Following is the list of archetypes in *The Hero's Journey*:

Hero – (from the Greek roots, heros and servos, meaning "to protect and serve") is willing to sacrifice his own needs on behalf of others, like a shepherd who will sacrifice to protect and serve his flock, is on a quest in pursuit of the internal grail which is one's self, essence, true nature.

Mentor – a wise voice, aids or trains the hero, teaches and protects heroes and gives them gifts, often speaks in the voice of a god, or is inspired by divine wisdom.

Threshold Guardian – an obstacle on the road to adventure, presents a menacing face to the hero, but if understood, can be overcome, bypassed, or turned into an ally, role is to test the hero.

Herald – a messenger, issues challenge to the hero, announces the coming of significant change--the *Call to Adventure.*

Shapeshifter – both sides of a mask, throws the hero off center, misleads, shifts in appearance and/or mood, loyalty and sincerity in question, unstable, surfaces doubt in the hero but has the ability to see the potential in everything and everyone.

Shadow – the dark, unconscious side, often unexpressed, unrealized or rejected aspects of one's self, often dedicated to the death, destruction, or defeat of the hero, sometimes an ally but is after the same goal as the hero and uses different tactics, challenges the hero and is a worthy opponent in the struggle, forces the hero to rise to the challenge.

Trickster – a comical sidekick, embodies the energies of mischief and desire for change, provides comic relief for the hero on the journey, points out folly and hypocrisy, draws attention to the imbalance or absurdity of a stagnant psychological situation, brings needed perspective to a situation that is just too serious.

Ally – An ally is a friend and helper of the hero, helping him to achieve his story goal. A special ally is the sidekick.

(Adapted from *The Writer's Journey* by Chris Vogler)

One more archetype is included in the particular *Hero's Journey* that is your path through prison:

> *Outlaw* – rebel, revolutionary, wild man; wants to overturn what isn't working in a situation; strategy is revenge or revolution; challenges conventional wisdom that hero has bought into; is comfortable with conflict and struggle, prefers it over the status quo.

We invite you on this rich and so rewarding human journey of—yourself and your story.

LESSON ONE

THE ORDINARY WORLD, YOUR STORY'S GENRE, & YOUR WRITING LIFE

THE ELDERLY COUPLE SAT ON THE BACK PORCH of their ranch house--eating applesauce and chatting. For three pages. Three long pages. What could I tell the writer about how to fix her opening? Throw it out, that's what.

A character wakes up in the morning, stretches, and sees the bright sun streaming through the window—if he has a window. Otherwise, it's the ringing of the alarm clock. Do you have any idea how many times I've read this same opening or one like it in, maybe, a thousand different manuscripts?

Is there a more crucial scene than the opening scene when it comes to engaging the reader in the drama that is your story? *The Hero's Journey* calls your opening scene *The Ordinary World*, and it must fulfill several different functions. In this lesson we'll look at each of those functions.

STAGE ONE: THE ORDINARY WORLD

THE ORDINARY WORLD IS THE HERO'S HOME TURF, containing his background, all that he is up until the point of entering the special world. He may or may not have the resources and support he needs to slay the dragons he'll meet in the special world, but if he doesn't, he'll acquire them once he gets there. The hero's ordinary world and the special world of the story should be very different although the hero will recognize similarities, because while he is learning new lessons in the special world, he may have been presented with them in *The Ordinary World* and been too weak or unwilling to respond. These similarities foreshadow the special world and its challenges.

A story opening must accomplish six things: 1) introduce the hero and his major goal and conflict, 2)) hook the reader, 3) introduce the story's major setting, 4) introduce the story's overall tone/emotion and create a mood, 5) point with suspense to where the story is going, and 6) at least hint at the story's theme/dramatic question.

One way to hook the reader and begin to engage him in the story is to introduce the high stakes for the hero at the beginning of his adventure. Consider what your hero has to gain or lose and find a way to present this, either in the dialogue, action, or narrative. Another way is to create a mood that emotionally engages the reader. Your hero's adventure should provoke some kind of emotion for him which should then transfer to the reader. If he's betrayed by a friend, he will be angry. If he's abandoned by a lover, sad (and angry). If he's stalked by a killer, afraid. There are a gamut of emotions you can use to begin to create the mood in your *Ordinary World* that will then carry over into the hero's adventure.

Some writers think that the way to engage a reader is to create an exotic setting for the hero, but if the setting is too exotic, the reader won't resonate with it. You want to create a balance between the unfamiliar, in order to keep things interesting, and the familiar so as to get the reader to connect with the hero. This is a balance you'll want to maintain throughout the story.

The tricky part of creating the hero's *Ordinary World* is that it's sometimes rather mundane; at home with his family eating dinner or playing board games, in the classroom at school, in his office. Not very exciting stuff. It's your job as the writer to create tension around something happening in *The Ordinary World* while simultaneously building suspense for what's to come in the special world. This is a great place to foreshadow what your hero may be up against as he moves into his adventure.

The Ordinary World presents a dramatic question that the story then proceeds to provide insight into through the dramatic action. For a genre story, the question can be as simple as: Will the cops catch up with the bad guys before they blow up one more bank (action-adventure)? Or: Will the detective find the killer (mystery)? For a mainstream or literary story, the question is more complicated: Will the outlaw/hero find reconciliation inside of himself for all of the wrongs done to him? Or: Will the hero choose to confront his internal demons now that he's in prison and is faced with them every single day as his fellow inmates mirror them for him?

Theme. This word seems to create a degree of anxiety in the hearts of the bravest writers. Why is that? Is it because we start our stories, not sure where we're going? Well, so? Isn't that one reason many of us write, to find out where we're going and what we think about where we're going? To discover the underlying purpose of what we're doing and who we are in our life's journey? A story's theme is simply its universal truth--an internal struggle and subsequent insight the reader can recognize and identify with as his own.

How is the hero's Ordinary World and the special world different? How are they the same?

What is your story's mood and how will you introduce it into The Ordinary World?

What are the high stakes for the hero?

What is your story's overall setting?

How will you create tension in The Ordinary World while building suspense for what's to come in the special world?

What is your story's dramatic question?

What is your story's theme, at least what you know of it?

CHOOSING YOUR GENRE

THERE ARE AS MANY GENRES AND COMBINATION OF GENRES for writing your *Hero's Journey* story as there are stories in your head. Any of the following can be written as a fictional short story, a novel, a personal experience short story, or a memoir. It's up to you. How much do you have to say? How deeply do you want to explore yourself, your outlaw archetype, and the external pivotal events of your life?

These are your choices:

1. *Mainstream ~ twentieth-century stories intended for the general public rather than a specific audience; challenges belief systems, suggests a new vision, asks questions, provokes introspection, shakes up rules*

2. *Literary ~ avant-garde, experimental, and exploratory stories, often incorporating unconventional and non-traditional writing style and techniques*

3. *Romance ~ stories focused on the development of the love relationship between the hero and heroine, the tension that pulls them together and/or drives them apart*

4. *Science Fiction / Fantasy ~ stories showing the effects of science, technology, and social and psychological theories on characters in the future/stories about magical or alternate worlds and kingdoms, using witches, warlocks, dragons and other myth-like creatures*

5. *Action / Adventure ~ fast-paced stories that put the characters at risk or in physical danger; includes thrilling near-misses and courageous and daring feats*

6. *Horror ~ stories designed to terrify the reader with pursuit and escape type plots, often using supernatural or demonic beings or characters with occult powers*

7. *Mystery ~ plot-driven stories with the emphasis on solving a crime of some kind; involves a series of clues leading to answers, rising tension and often increasing danger as the resolution is approached*

8. *Suspense Thrillers ~ stories that develop a physical and/or psychological threat to the main character, includes a dark character that the protagonist must escape or overcome*

9. *Historical ~ stories taking place in a factual historical time; characters are dropped into real historical events and interact with real historical people as kings and queens; westerns are centered in the old American West with characters from that time; i.e. cowboys, Indians, settlers, miners, etc.*

10. *Religious / Spiritual Novels ~ spiritual and message-driven stories using characters in conflict with good and evil, externally and internally; new age stories that deal with some aspect of the paranormal and/or psychic world*

11. *Comedic~ stories with an emphasis on the humorous or satirical aspects of the story*

12. *Philosophical ~ stories that make a point about life's meaning; can be allegories or express political ideas; deal with pressing social concerns of a certain period*

13. *War ~ stories set in the middle of war; emphasis is on the battles won and lost and the heroism involved*

14. *Juvenile / Young Adult~ stories featuring a young protagonist in any of the above categories*

It's up to you. This is not an exhaustive list, by the way, but these are the main categories. You may not know what kind of story you're writing, which genre, and you may not care. That's fine, too. But if you want to be more intentional as to the type of story you're writing, the above will serve as a pretty thorough list.

YOUR WRITING LIFE

Signing up for this course means at least for right now, you have taken on the role of a writer. You can start calling yourself that. It's one of the first lessons I learned as a new writer from an editor who spoke at a writers conference I attended early on in my writing career. The criteria for being a writer is not getting your work published—that's where you earn the title of *author*. No, a *writer* is simply a person who writes.

To take on the writing life means any number of things. It means to become curious, to start listening more than talking, to set goals for what you want to accomplish as a writer, to write something every day, to begin to nurture your creative self, to start showing your writing to others and to take in as much feedback as you can.

You're in a prison, so I don't know how much you can alter your daily schedule, but as much as possible, make sure at least some of every day revolves around your writing. If you can get any quiet at all (yeah, right!), ponder your story ideas, see how many of them are begging to be developed, sit down and write. Or stand up and write. Do what you have to do. Many works of brilliance have been penned while someone was in prison; e.g. *Don Quixote* by Miguel de Cervantes, *Pilgrim's Progress* by John Bunyan, *De Profundis* by Oscar Wilde, *Civil Disobedience* by Henry David Thoreau, and *Long Walk to Freedom* by Nelson Mandela, just to name a few. Mandela wrote to his wife, Winnie, from prison: "The cell is an ideal place to learn to know yourself."

To live the writing life means to begin to think like a writer. It's to become curious. Remember what we talked about in the Intro, how the outside world is closed off to you right now, and how it's time to explore your internal landscape in the same way an explorer would search out a new world. You may think you know yourself, but I can guarantee that you don't know yourself nearly as well as you could if you were to dive into your inner landscape and start poking around. Do you ever wonder where the outlaw part of yourself comes from? The hero part? The explorer part? These are all parts of who you are as a man and a human being, just waiting for you to become curious enough to ask the kinds of questions that will allow a deeper measure of those archetypes to emerge and begin to develop within you. Writing a hero's journey story is an ideal way to begin to approach the parts of yourself you don't yet know as it's a story that's already written. You have only to be the channel, to give that story a voice. The interesting part is that you don't have just one story in you—you have many. All you have to decide for now is which one you want to explore for the purpose of this course.

What are the tools a writer needs? Hey, if you have paper and a few pencils, you have all of the tools you need to be a writer. Well, access to a typewriter or computer would help, so don't get thrown in the hole during this course and get that privilege taken away.

Maybe more important than tools are the attributes a writer needs in order to sustain a writing career. A writer needs:

- *a degree of integrity, not just with his readers, but with himself. There's no point in making a decision to be a writer if you're a liar—lying to others, lying to yourself. It's not a matter of writing the factual truth about everything in your story for this course, but it is a matter of knowing that you're being honest with yourself about the truth in your story.*

- *some kind of work ethic (I prefer work ethic to the word, discipline, which most writers rebel against). You have to know deep down that becoming diligent as a writer is going to benefit you in some way, achieve for you at least a measure of success of some kind.*

- *passion for the ideas that come up and the insight to know which ones to pursue. There's no such thing as a "bad" idea, really, but if you're not ready to execute it, it's not going to work for you at that particular time. The degree of passion you have for an idea is a good clue whether or not that's one you should pursue.*

- *the confidence to use your authentic voice in your writing, however that voice emerges; no censoring, no judging, no pushing against your unique voice.*

The rest you can learn. You can learn how to structure a story. Whether deciding to write a novel or a memoir, you can learn how to develop fictional characters or how to bring real people to life on the page. You can learn to describe a setting so that it's three-dimensional or to create the kind of tension and suspense that holds the reader in the story. You can do this.

Following is a list of questions designed for you to consider the writing part of yourself and make some decisions on a daily basis. The best time to fill out this sheet is right after you finish your writing for the day, or if you didn't write, before you go to bed at night.

WRITING DECISIONS

Date

_____

Did I write today? If so, what? If not, why not?

How many words or pages did I write today?

How long did I write today?

Did anything hinder me before I started? What did it take to motivate me?

Do I feel good about what I wrote? Do I feel good about having written? Why or why not?

What do I plan to write tomorrow?

ASSIGNMENT:

1) Write a dramatic scene or a narrative summary of your hero's *Ordinary World*. (A hero and a protagonist are one and the same, to be used interchangeably, but for the sake of the course, the protagonist will now be known as the hero.) In this assignment you will be introducing your story's overall setting, mood, dramatic question, conflict, and theme, as well as the high stakes if your character is not able to achieve the goal you've set for him. A dramatic scene is full of action and dialogue as well as narrative.

Please keep your assignment at 1000 or fewer words. If you're writing a short story or short personal experience story, that shouldn't be a problem. Of course, if you're writing a memoir or a novel, you can't submit all of the scenes it might take to get yourself or your character through *The Ordinary World*. You can use this course to plan your story or to submit some of your scenes that reveal the progression of the story. You will usually have to compress your scenes in order to stay under the word limits. So, you can choose one of the following options:

- Write a short scene of 1000 words

- Write one short scene and a summary of the other scenes in *The Ordinary World*

- Write a summary of all of the scenes in *The Ordinary World*

2) Write a 200-word paragraph describing your story's genre (horror, action-adventure, fantasy, etc.) and type (memoir, novel, short story, etc.) and why you've chosen that specific genre and type.

3) Write a 600-word bio paragraph about what you know about the storyteller archetype that you're now going to allow free reign, the writing life you're now going to engage in, and the writer that you now are. Describe your passion for your story, your integrity as a writer, your work ethic as an adult, at least to this point. What is your confidence level when it comes to yourself as a writer? Do you resonate with the word, outlaw, hero, explorer or all of these, and how will you explore these in your story? Are you curious about yourself, about others, about how different humans approach their lives on this planet? Describe the writing life as you now know it with you in the center.

LESSON TWO

THE CALL TO ADVENTURE, CREATING COOL CHARACTERS/ARCHETYPES, & WRITING YOUR STORY SUMMARY

"READY OR NOT, HERE I COME!" Remember that line from the game of Tag in your childhood? If you've never heard of Tag, sigh, you're very young. It was this interactive game kids played in the fifties and sixties before video games. We actually played it outside in the street rather than in front of a television or computer screen. I can hardly imagine it. Anyway, the person who was IT counted to a hundred, and everyone else hid. "...ninety-eight, ninety-nine, one hundred. Ready or not, here I come!" We hoped we were ready, but that line always struck fear in our hearts as the one who was IT was now coming after us.

The Call to Adventure is like that. Ready or not, the herald archetype appears, and the hero's only choice is how he's going to respond. He has a choice whether to go on the adventure or not, but if he doesn't go, he becomes a tragic hero and the story is pretty much over before it really gets started, certainly before the hero learns anything or there's any redemption. The outlaw archetype may rise up when the hero receives the call—either internally or showing up as another character--and cause a hero to take a temporary detour, going on an adventure that leads him to commit a crime, but a true hero will eventually wake up to how the outlaw archetype wants to play out in his life and begin to integrate it rather than let it drive him from within.

If you're writing a novel or memoir, it may have taken you several scenes to get through your *Ordinary World*, but *The Call to Adventure* should occur at least by the end of Chapter One. If you're writing a short story or short personal experience story, we should reach *The Call to Adventure* at the end of the first scene.

STAGE TWO: THE CALL TO ADVENTURE

SO YOU'VE INTRODUCED THE HERO'S ORDINARY WORLD, and the herald (see Ch. 4 for description) announces *The Call to Adventure*, otherwise known as the "inciting incident." This is the moment the story's action kicks into a higher gear. Something is starting to happen. The hero's external and internal goals begin to become clear at this point—the action plays out externally, but the true hero also understands that the real journey is an internal one, a journey of human transformation. Here is where he gets a glimpse of the stakes of the game. Will he achieve the dream, survive the journey, confront the challenge, transcend the ego, be able to transform his life? These are the questions being asked of our hero that the story will then attempt to address.

Ready or Not. *The Call to Adventure* isn't often something the hero has planned. It can come to him because something in his life is no longer working. Something rocks his perception of himself and his world. Something happens that he can no longer tolerate, and he sets out to change it. It could be that the hero suddenly loses something or someone—a job, his health, a loved one. As I mentioned above, for the outlaw, the *Call* could initially mean committing a crime, but even while unconscious of it at the time, the outlaw's soul knows the next step he needs to take on his human journey, and so appeals to his higher nature, eventually leading him to prison and his ultimate redemption.

I remember a dark night when someone (the herald disguised as my son) showed up at my door. I looked out the peephole, and I intuitively knew, as much as I'd ever known anything, that this was my *Call to Adventure*. It would be the beginning of a *Hero's Journey* that I would never, ever have chosen for myself. I was a reluctant hero when my son's two years of substance abuse and ongoing homelessness began. Unwittingly, he was my herald. Externally, my life became about looking for my son on every downtown street, sometimes at midnight, waiting for the phone to ring and my son to check in, my heart leaping when he'd show up, my heart sinking as he would walk away again into the night, his backpack fading into the darkness, my eyes stinging with tears once more. Internally? I was being called to surrender him to his own life's purpose rather than mine for him in a way I never had before. My dreams, my hopes, my desires for who he could become (pursuing his art, going to art school) sank to the bottom of my heart, and I had to content myself with the simple joy of learning that he had survived one more night on the streets.

The *Call* usually takes the hero by surprise. Nothing will be the same for him ever again. It may disturb him, trouble him, disorient him. It often calls into question everything that's important to him.

You may still be blaming the arresting officer, the prosecutor, or the judge for your fate, but even though it may feel like it at times, you're not a victim of your human existence. Your venture into the prison system, though certainly not a conscious decision on your part, is at some level, a choice you've made and your personal *Call to Adventure*. You can resist or you can surrender to it.

What is your hero's external Call to Adventure? Internal?

How does the herald show up announcing the Call?

What is your hero doing when he receives his Call?

Does the hero see the Call to Adventure coming? What is the most surprising part of this moment for him?

How does the Call to Adventure appeal to the outlaw in the hero?

CREATING COOL CHARACTERS/ARCHETYPES

EVERY STORY HAS A CAST OF CHARACTERS—real or fictional. It's the people in our stories that engage the reader in the plot or story line. And so it's your job, as the writer, to ensure that your characters are three-dimensional, fascinating, believable, authentic, and fully dramatized. What causes a reader to remember a story is not so much what the characters did but who they became as they did what they did. Actor Robert Redford has said that when considering a new project to direct or produce, he looks for those scripts where a character is somehow transformed as the story plays out.

Character development isn't as important in a plot-driven story such as in the horror or action/adventure genres, but I personally believe that many plot-driven stories would more effectively communicate with readers if they included character transformation. Of course, in the character-driven story, the development of the character is crucial to the story itself. In many cases, it's the whole story.

In thinking about your story's archetypes, you want to consider how to develop characters so that they connect with readers in a way that is memorable and will impact them on an emotional level. You'll need a hero (if you're writing a memoir, that's you), a shadow (to oppose the hero and provide a mirror), a herald (to announce the journey), a threshold guardian (to block the hero's way), a shapeshifter (to keep the hero off balance), a trickster (to offer another perspective to the hero) and an ally (to offer support and encouragement), all of whom will either cheer or oppose the hero's progress on his journey as he pursues his goal. The outlaw archetype isn't one that Joseph Campbell or Chris Vogler ever overtly discussed, but because this archetype often functions outside of the law, as you well know, it includes aspects of the shadow archetype. If you identify strongly with the outlaw archetype, and since at the present time at least, you have to call a prison cell your "house," it could be that your shadow/outlaw and hero might almost be one and the same character in your story. At least they will

The Outlaw Archetype

Motto: Rules are made to be broken

Core desire: Revenge or revolution

Goal: To overturn or destroy what isn't working for himself or for society

Fear: To be powerless, trivialized, inconsequential, or ineffectual

Strategy: To disrupt, destroy, or shock

Weakness: To cross over to the dark side, criminality

Gift: Outrageousness, radical freedom

Otherwise known as: Rebel, revolutionary, wild man, misfit, iconoclast

share some common aspects: the hero part—the need to protect himself and his loved ones, a desire to transform dark parts of his personality into light, the courage to continue to engage with the journey no matter how difficult the external or internal terrain; the outlaw part--a compulsion to pursue a goal, whether or not it's legal, a tendency to resist authority to effect social change, an unconscious desire to go against conventional wisdom.

Whether we're writing fiction or a true personal experience story, it's often how the characters in our stories interact with and influence the main character that determines the outcome of the major conflict, whatever it is. In this sense, the roles we give our characters are very important. In order to create three-dimensional characters, we must know them well before we put them into our stories. This is the reason you want to spend some time pondering and developing only those characters who are necessary to the plot and who will best assist the major character in communicating the story's theme.

Your main task when developing the characters for your story is to think through each character's role. Certainly, you want to know each character's physical characteristics; eye color, hair color, body shape, gestures and mannerisms, etc. You want to know who the character's family is, where he lives, what his hobbies are. Then you want to develop his internals: his dreams and longings, his obsessions and addictions, his goals and motivations. More specifically, you want to know each character's background, fatal flaw, major conflict, belief system, and deepest wound (all to be explained more fully in Chapter Three). What would your character's perfect day look like? Be creative.

The three most important things to know about any character are: 1) what he wants, 2) what he fears , and 3) what will make him most memorable to the reader.

These are the three things that will engage a reader in your story and compel him to read from beginning to end. You want to consider these three things for every character on both the external and internal level because our stories should be both external and internal.

This is not all something you have to think through completely right now, as your characters emerge as you write them into the story. You get to know them as the story unfolds for you. But you do want to at least give them a little thought, especially in how they function in your *Hero's Journey* through the story.

We'll be going into more depth on each of the eight archetypes in future lessons, but for now, if you need to refresh your mind on each of their roles, go back to our Introduction and reread the list.

WRITING YOUR STORY SUMMARY

IN THIS, OUR SECOND CHAPTER, you'll be given the opportunity to write a story summary so that you can think through what you initially see your story as being about. Who are your characters and what are they doing? Who are they becoming? What is the plot about? How much do you know about your theme before you start writing? A story summary should be short, maybe just a few hundred words. This isn't the kind of synopsis you'd ever send to an editor. It's simply a narrative description of the story as you know it so far.

You don't have to think your story all the way through before you begin to write. That's what the writing is for. If you knew everything that was going to happen to your hero, would you really want to write the story? You want to have the option of changing anything along the way. So what you write today in a summary may not even resemble what the story ends up being. That's okay. We just want to give you the opportunity to get something down on paper, and it gives us the opportunity to get a sense of where you want to take your story. (By the way, if at any time during the course, you want to change stories midstream, that's not a problem. Just one caveat—you'll need to start from where we are in the course at the time.)

ASSIGNMENT:

1) Write a dramatic scene or a narrative summary of your hero's *Call to Adventure*. Make sure you identify the herald, and in some way, show how he announces your hero's *Call*. Reveal how the hero responds, both externally and internally.

Please keep your assignment at 1000 or fewer words. As we discussed in the previous lecture, if you're writing a short story or short personal experience story, that shouldn't be a problem, but if you're writing a memoir or a novel, you can't submit all of the scenes it might take to get yourself or your character through the *Call to Adventure* stage. You can use this course to: 1) plan your story, 2) get feedback on scenes that reveal the progression of your story, or 3) get feedback on certain scenes you feel aren't working, with which you need extra help. You may have to compress your scenes in order to stay under the word limits. So, please choose one of the following options:

- *Write a short Call to Adventure scene of 1000 words*
- *Write one scene and a summary of the other scenes in the Call to Adventure*
- *Write a summary of all of the scenes in the Call to Adventure*

2) Create your cast of characters in 500 or fewer words. Name each character and describe in a sentence or brief paragraph, not the character's appearance, but the archetype and how that archetype either supports or opposes the hero's goal and agenda, whether it's external or internal (preferably both).

3) Write a 500-word summary for the story you want to work on in this course. You can probably only include a brief description of your hero,

maybe the antagonist, but try to focus on the plot (what happens) if you're writing a genre story, or the character arc (how the hero is transformed) if you're writing a mainstream or literary fictional story or memoir.

LESSON THREE

THE REFUSAL OF THE CALL,
THE ROLE OF THE HERO
& CREATING YOUR STORY'S VOICE & VIEWPOINT

ONE OF MY FAVORITE *REFUSAL OF THE CALL* SCENES is the one in the Wizard of Oz where Dorothy, the lion, the scarecrow, and the tin man are about to enter the castle, and the lion says, "Wait a minute, fellahs. I was just thinkin'. I really don't want to see the Wizard this much. I better wait for you outside."

When Dorothy tries to encourage the lion, assuring him that the Wizard is going to give him some courage, he says, "I'd be too scared to ask for it." After a lot of coaxing, his final line is, "Oh, I want to go home, I want to go home."

Some might argue that this is the *Refusal of the Call* for the lion because it's so far into the story, but then he's not the hero either. He's an ally. No matter. Each character has his or her own journey, and this is the lion refusing his.

Not too many outlaw/hero types are going to acknowledge their fears as readily as the lion does here, let alone allow anyone else to see them. But your inner outlaw knows what's most scary for you, and as a true hero, you want to grow in your insight into the fears that might hold you back on your *Hero's Journey*. Keep in mind that a hero can only exercise courage in the face of fear. Without fear, there is no courage.

STAGE THREE: REFUSAL OF THE CALL

IN REAL LIFE, WE REFUSE *CALLS TO ADVENTURE* ALL OF THE TIME. As children, when asked to perform in front of an audience, whether it's playing a musical instrument, acting in a dramatic production, or participating in a sport, at some point, we stomp our feet and refuse to go forward. When it's time to get married or have our first child, we get cold feet. Some of us refuse and keep refusing all of our lives, becoming more and more afraid to take risks. Our lives become a series of missed opportunities. In a story, when a hero refuses a call, it's temporary. If it wasn't, we would have to call him a tragic hero, and the story would end right there.

Isn't that what a hero is—someone who moves ahead on the *Journey* in the face of fear? So when fear is present, for many of us, the first tendency is to run. The hero may resist just once, or if his fear is intense, he may persist in his reluctance. The more he resists, the more the reader understands that for the hero, this adventure is a very big deal, a risky venture. For the outlaw/hero, the fear often has a larger scope—not a fear of crocodiles, though it could be that, but a fear of, say, a societal issue against which he must plant his feet and refuse to move. Henry David Thoreau was an outlaw/hero in 1849 when he wrote his essay, *Civil Disobedience*; he refused to pay the poll tax imposed by a government that continued to tolerate slavery.

When the hero is afraid of the journey, it's sometimes because he's been previously wounded, burned, hurt in some way. He needs a new motivation, to be infused with passion anew. A new motivation could come in the form of something he could stand to lose if he doesn't accept the call (a job, a lover, a friend). What will raise the stakes for your hero, making him accept the journey ahead?

If the hero refuses the *Call to Adventure* and keeps refusing, he could face some serious consequences. Some opportunities come around, and if we don't grab them, they don't come around again. If we resist a *Call*, sometimes it weakens the fiber of our very being, making it that much harder to accept the *Call* if it does come around again.

In one sense, this entire stage of the journey typifies the hero as outlaw. Because it's often in the *Refusal of the Call* that the outlaw archetype shows up in the hero. If the hero is as much outlaw as he is hero in, say, that the story's theme has to do with a necessary revolt against society, then this stage is central to the story as a whole. And the outlaw archetype is now driving the plot as much as is the hero because his resistance is what the story is all about.

Sometimes heroes are called to more than one adventure at a time, and they have to choose. A hero may have to choose between a lover/family (one adventure) and a career (another adventure). The direction of the story is determined by which journey the hero chooses.

Not all heroes are reluctant. Some are motivated and ready to go—and in denial of the dangers waiting for them. In that case, others have to warn the hero of those very real dangers. My grown daughter once decided to adopt a child with special needs. She was motivated and ready to go. But in her naiveté, she thought she was only bringing a little friend into her home. I felt like the constant naysayer (and threshold guardian) there for a while as I warned and warned. Still, she had no idea and was shocked at what the real adventure turned out to be.

Oftentimes others clutch at and cling to the hero when he's about to go on his adventure. Threshold guardians appear at this point, as the hero is already weakened by his own insecurities and fears; threshold guardians pick up on that and can prey on it.

Back Story

At some point, you'll have to begin to build your hero's back story--all the relevant information about a character's history and background. You want to get past the *Ordinary World* and *Call to Adventure* before you start to overwhelm the reader with what happened in the character's past. Your first task is to hook the reader in the hero's major dramatic conflict, then the reader will be interested in what brought your hero to this point. So bring the back story in as it becomes relevant to the conflict you're developing. The *Refusal of the Call* is often a good place to introduce the back story because it can reveal your hero's motivation, why he may be less than eager to go on the adventure.

Some stories need a lot of back story, some not so much. The more internal your story is, the more back story you'll need. Very important: you don't want to dump the back story on the reader all at once. Provide bits and pieces as the hero moves from place to place, either from within his thoughts as he's reminded of something or in dialogue as he's blurting out parts of his past to other characters. The character himself determines how much back story to reveal. Is he a private person or is he someone who loves to tell anyone who will listen about everything that's happened in his past? Is he a character who tries to forget it or does he tend to obsess on it?

What are the hero's excuses for refusing the Call?

How has the hero been previously wounded? What is his resistance about? What will motivate him once again?

Does the hero face consequences for refusing the Call? What are they?

Does the hero face two conflicting Calls? What happens?

Is your hero willing? How do others in his life warn him of the dangers?

Who tries to hold your hero back from his adventure during his Refusal of the Call?

What is the part of the hero's back story that would cause him to refuse the Call? Does he talk easily about his past, or is he reluctant to reveal his secrets?

THE ROLE OF THE HERO

Hero energy:

• shows up as positive and redemptive

• transcends the bounds and illusions of the ego

• represents the ego's search for identity and wholeness

• reveals the soul in transformation and the journey each person takes through life

• expresses universal traits and motivations— admirable and not-so admirable

• possesses a fatal flaw powerful enough to destroy

• is willing or unwilling (temporarily) but committed

THE HERO IS YOUR STORY'S PROTAGONIST. According to Chris Vogler in *The Writer's Journey*, "a hero is someone who is willing to sacrifice his own needs on behalf of others." That is definitely true, but even more importantly, in my estimation, is that a hero is someone who is awakening to his own life journey, becoming conscious as to his purpose on the planet. Joseph Campbell calls it *finding your bliss*.

According to the human personality study called the Enneagram (something else you can study in your spare time), every human being is driven by one of nine universal human motivations; to be right, to be loved, to succeed, to find significance, to understand and be understood, to be safe, to be happy, to be strong/self-reliant, and to have peace/avoid conflict. Choose which of these motivations is most important to your hero, and you have the key to all that drives him in your story. The hero's primary motivation begins in childhood and is most often the result of a wound he receives; a parent's death, the loss of a pet, violent physical or sexual abuse, a house fire, witnessing violence, anything that traumatizes our hero.

The wound informs our hero's motivation and creates a want in his psyche, his goal in the story. What he wants should be both external and internal. He's pursuing something outside of himself, which is the plot, while developing his inner self, which is the transformation that results because of the courage he has to find to sustain his external pursuit. I created a mini-hero's journey for myself when I bought a motorcycle and then had to learn to ride it—my goal. Every day, I lived with fear until I rode that day. I learned a lot about myself as, daily, I had to find the courage to keep riding until it became second nature. External and internal. My motorcycle adventure illustrates in a small way how to create the journey for your hero. Normally, a hero's goal is much larger.

Your hero needs a conflict in the story, something that makes it seem impossible for him to reach his goal. Again, the conflict should be both external and internal and should include a moment when he faces his greatest fear connected to his goal. So, for example, if your hero's goal is to be a concert pianist, but he can't afford a piano or music lessons, and everyone around him is laughing at him, telling him to get a sensible job, what is his greatest fear? That they're all right? That he doesn't have musical talent? That he'll never be able to fulfill his dream and so will have a meaningless life? He must confront his fear and do battle with it in a scene.

Every hero needs a *fatal flaw*. This is a character trait that has the power to sabotage him from the inside and render him incapable of achieving his goal. The *fatal flaw* often originates from something that happened in his childhood, a major disappointment or betrayal in his young life, an event or moment that he internalized. This traumatic event creates a *psychic wound* for our hero and so now drives him on the inside—sometimes consciously, most often unconsciously. This wound could show up physically, but it doesn't have to. This is all part of developing your hero in a way that's focused for the sake of storytelling. In real life, most of us have more than one fatal flaw and psychic wound that are capable of paralyzing us so that we can't reach our goals or develop as human beings. It's up to us how hard we want to work to heal our wounds and continue to grow. Unless you're working with a tragic hero, the hero in your story doesn't have the option of growing or not—he's in a story so he must keep moving forward. Chris Vogler speaks of the "missing piece" in your hero's personality, say, the ability to trust again, or to find the voice he may have lost as a child. This, too, can show up in a physical way. What is missing from your hero's physical world? What has he lost? What's missing in a hero's life gives the reader sympathy for him and causes her to emotionally connect with him because she's lost something, too. It might be a family member or a material possession that has great meaning to the hero. In some way, he's incomplete and needs to find a way to feel whole again.

True heroes are not victims but are active in their journeys. Too many "young" writers have another character or some magical being swoop down to save the hero at his point of greatest need. While other characters definitely play a part in the hero's rescue, ultimately, the hero must *do* something to save himself. Consider what you want your character to *do* to bring about a satisfying conclusion to his journey.

Though I don't think it's the purest definition of the hero, true heroes do make sacrifices for the good of others. The most misunderstood type of hero, in my opinion, is the outlaw/hero. You may or may not think you deserve to be in prison. You may be creating a fictional outlaw/hero who sees himself differently than how others see him. But as the writer of the story, it's your task to present the outlaw/hero in such a way that the reader can understand his perspective because you have taken her deeply enough inside of his head so that she recognizes her own outlaw/hero archetype. What are the sacrifices your hero is making even though others may not understand or perceive them as sacrifices?

In some way in the story, the hero confronts death. This could occur simultaneously with the moment he faces off with his greatest fear. Think about the kind of death you want your hero to face that will bring about the greatest transformation. This moment could mean facing a death to a part of his personality, the death of a loved one, the death of a dream, his own physical death. (But please don't kill off your hero; a dead man tells no tales. This is another young writer's mistake—killing off the hero.)

The reader begins to form an opinion of your hero in the very first scene in which he appears. What is your hero doing when he makes his first appearance? What is he wearing? What is coming from him in the way of demeanor, attitude, energy? Is he the sole viewpoint character, or do you plan to use other viewpoints? This is a big decision for the writer. You want to consider if the story belongs to your hero alone. If you have a large theme, sometimes you want to show the perspectives of other characters to more fully explore the aspects of that theme. Will you use an intimate first-person point of view or third-person that gives you a little distance? (Please don't mix first and third person—yes, you'll see this in a few published works, but it's a violation of the unity of a story.)

As much as is possible, you want your reader to connect with your hero, to identify with him as he searches for the treasure that is his goal and slays his dragons along the way. So when he makes his first appearance, what

---

Hero's purpose:
Internal:

• to represent the human spirit in positive action while showing the consequences of weakness and reluctance to act

• to reveal human vulnerability; challenged to overcome inner doubts, errors in thinking, guilt, or past trauma

• to express humankind's universal drives; to be important, understood, free, safe, successful, independent, secure, loved

• to integrate all of the separate parts of a personality into one complete, balanced entity

will cause your reader to make that vital connection? What is happening in the opening scene that will bring out his humanness and vulnerability?

Your hero may be excited and willing to go on the journey from the first moment the herald announces it. Or not. As we discussed above, some heroes are reluctant, scared, shy, unmotivated, holding back. The reluctant hero must at some point find his motivation and commit to the journey. It's your job as the writer to discover what will give him that necessary kick in the butt that moves him forward.

There are two other kinds of hero—the *tragic hero* and *the anti-hero*. The tragic hero is a protagonist who agrees to go on the journey but learns little, if anything, along the way. He cops in some way at the end and remains unchanged, his goal forgotten, his demons still very much alive and tormenting him. In the *Hero's Journey* that is prison, this is the man who, instead of using this time set aside to heal his psychic wound, holes up in his cell plotting his next rape and murder when he gets out. This is the character who gives up the dream, aborting his journey, because it's too hard and goes back to working at the hamburger joint. Tragic heroes make for sad endings to stories, so only let your hero go this way if it best serves your theme and if it's true to who the character is at the conclusion of the story.

Traditionally, the anti-hero is the kind of story protagonist who goes about pursuing his goal in an unconventional and anti-societal (or anti-social) way. This character often hasn't been civilized in the way others have been and so what others think of him is far down on his list of priorities. He's usually an outlaw in the true sense of the word, misunderstood by society. We are all a combination of both light and dark, and he may be a character whose light side is in need of development. An anti-hero can fly by the seat of his pants, neglecting to inquire or reflect on himself and what his role in society really is, and so the ending of a story about an anti-hero wakes us up, revealing what we can learn about ourselves if we neglect to inquire into or reflect on how our behavior contributes (or not) in a redemptive way to the world around us.

Which of the nine universal drives is motivating your hero?

What is your hero's external goal? Internal?

Hero's purpose:
External:

• to give the reader a window into the story

• to give the reader a character with whom to identify

• to overcome obstacles and achieve goals, to attain wisdom and knowledge; to be the learner in the story

• to take action; to perform the decisive action in the story, the action that takes the most risk and responsibility

• to sacrifice (make holy) something of value on behalf of an ideal of a group

• to transcend physical or metaphorical death

What is your hero's conflict about?

What is your hero's greatest fear?

What is you're hero's fatal flaw?

What is your hero's psychic wound?

What is your hero missing in his personality? What is missing from his external life?

What action does your hero perform to save himself and heal his wound?

What does your hero sacrifice?

What kind of death does your hero face?

Does your story's viewpoint belong to your hero alone, or will you use other viewpoints? If others, which ones?

How will you introduce your hero to the reader so that a connection is made? So that the reader can identify with him?

Is your hero excited about the journey ahead of him or is he dragging his feet? If he's reluctant, what will it take to motivate him?

Is your hero a tragic or anti-hero? What makes this true?

"Heroes are symbols of the soul in transformation, and of the journey each person takes through life. The stages of that progression, the natural stages of life and growth, make up *The Hero's Journey*."

~Chris Vogler

CREATING YOUR STORY'S VOICE & VIEWPOINT

CHOOSING YOUR STORY'S VIEWPOINT can be one of the most important parts of planning your story, yet so many writers seem to do it in a kind of random way, just taking off in either the first, third, or omniscient voice without a conscious reason for choosing that viewpoint.

But how do we decide? How do we know whether to use first, third, omniscient or a distant narrator's voice for our stories? Wouldn't it be nice if one of the characters spoke up to announce that he or she wanted to be the viewpoint character? Or if the next time, you sat down to work on your story, three or four of your characters stood up in your mind to let you know that they all had something to say?

At the risk of sounding a little out-there, that's sometimes how it does happen. Writing a story is more organic than we often realize, and if we're listening to our characters and listening to our own voice about the story, we'll receive messages about viewpoint along with theme and characters and everything else that goes into telling a story.

Since there are so many different kinds of stories, we could have quite the complex discussion on viewpoint. But I'd rather not complicate the discussion any more than we have to, and so let's keep our emphasis on the three major types of viewpoint; omniscient, third person and first person. There are variations of all of these, but these are our three choices for now.

Every story has its own viewpoint and voice and so let's take a look at the choices and see if we can narrow down the best choice for your story for this course.

EXPLORING YOUR STORY'S VIEWPOINT

YOU MAY WONDER ABOUT THE DIFFERENCE BETWEEN a story's viewpoint and its voice, and ten different writing coaches may offer that many answers to what the difference is. I would explain it this way. The story's viewpoint is its perception of the story events and the other characters, as well as the working out of the story's theme. To create your story's viewpoint is to choose a perception that will be as honest as possible about the truth you want to communicate in that story. A story's voice, on the other hand, feels more like the emotional perspective of the story, the emotional response to the story events once they've been perceived through the viewpoint.

I may be making this more complicated than it needs to be. What we're really talking about here is choosing the best character out of your cast of characters, the one who *holds* the story you want to tell. One character has the key to the truth. He usually doesn't know he has the key until you explore who he is through the story and he realizes it.

If the story is a factual one and you're exploring something that happened in your personal life, then of course the viewpoint is yours. Sometimes this is the point in the creative process where you decide on fiction or nonfiction. Thinking about telling a true story in one's own personal viewpoint, for example, scares some writers. But then writing a fictional account of a factual experience feels to some writers like they're copping out. It's up to you.

Sometimes a story's viewpoint emerges right away because you know whose story you want to tell. Other times, choosing the viewpoint can be a downright confusing process. Knowing what's driving your story may help with this process: stories are either character, plot, concept, or setting driven.

1) Character

The viewpoint usually rises up organically in the character-driven story. The character appears in your mind and simply wants to tell his story. Unless another character rises up beside him clamoring for a voice, you're home free. Now all you have to do is decide on the first or third person perspective.

2) Plot

Many plot-driven stories are written in dual or multiple viewpoints; this is for the purpose of creating maximum suspense from more than one perspective. Because many plot-driven stories don't have characters that express a lot of depth, the suspense in the story is driven by external plot events and so a variety of characters' reactions to these events is what creates a compelling ride for the reader.

3) Concept

Some stories are concept-driven, which means you start with theme instead of character, plot, or setting. When you start with theme, you can choose the character who has the largest conflict connected to your story's theme, or you can choose to tell the story from a few different viewpoints, if you'd like to reveal more than one perspective on the issue you want to discuss in your story.

4) Setting

When a story's setting is more prominent in your mind than anything else, you have to find the character within your cast who will interact with the setting most authentically and most intimately. This can be one character or a number of characters, determined by how much of a part the setting plays in the story and how deeply the characters are connected to the setting.

Famous Heroes:
Martin Luther King Jr.
Mother Teresa
Atticus Finch
Nelson Mandela
Bono
Michael Jackson (tragic hero)

Is your story character, plot, concept, or setting driven? Consider what's most important to you about the story you're writing for this course.

DISCOVERING YOUR STORY'S VOICE

OVER THE YEARS I HAVE WRITTEN literally hundreds of short stories, novels, personal experience stories and narrative nonfiction books. And every single time I have to carefully consider the voice I want to use, which will be the most effective approach to the story I want to tell.

There are no hard and fast rules about how to find your story's voice. I know some writers who sit down and start writing in a particular voice which then becomes a story as the pages begin to grow. The story organically evolves out of the writer's voice.

What happens to you emotionally when you think about or sit down to work on your story? Can you feel yourself tense up? Do you feel anger, fear, sorrow? Maybe it's just the opposite—you feel loose and free? Maybe you even feel like laughing at either yourself or your characters' quirks as you begin to write. Pay attention to how you feel as this will alert you to the authentic voice that wants to emerge as you write.

I wrote three-fourths of a novel one time in multiple viewpoint just because I wanted to explore three different characters—I thought. But it wasn't right, and I knew it. It didn't feel authentic, and my writing group agreed every time I read them a chapter. I finally realized that one of the major characters wanted to tell her story in the first person voice, and as soon as I started writing the story in first person, it took off and became almost too real. I was trying to keep a distance from my characters, but one of them wanted to be up close and personal and when I decided to let her, the story began to work on an entirely different level.

The voice makes the story what it is. Consider some of your favorite novels or memoirs and how different they would have been had the writer used a different voice. A melancholic character instead of an eccentric one. If the memoirist had approached her childhood abuse story satirically rather than so seriously. If the writer had used a Homer Simpson voice instead of a Simon Cowell or Al Sharpton voice.

Your story's voice is there waiting for you to hear it and then honor it.

CHOOSING YOUR STORY'S VIEWPOINT/VOICE

YOU HAVE THREE CHOICES when it comes to the perspective through which you want to tell your story: omniscient, first person, and third person.

OMNISCIENT:

The omniscient viewpoint is a third-person (he/she) perspective, one in which the reader is in all of the characters' heads at once or in no one's head at all. It's a panoramic view of all of the characters all of the time.

The omniscient viewpoint was used a lot more in the forties and fifties than it is now, but it's still often used in fantasy, science fiction, and some epic stories that have a huge cast. Oh, and in stories where the author doesn't know what he's doing. He may call the viewpoint for his story omniscient, but it can more accurately be called head-hopping. This author simply doesn't want to probe his characters deeply enough to discover whose story it is, or he really doesn't know much about viewpoint and just moves in and out of everyone's head on a whim.

The reason the omniscient viewpoint isn't often a good choice is because the reader can only emotionally identify with one character at a time, so when you move in and out of everyone's heads in a scene, the reader can't emotionally engage with anyone—not good. When you fail to engage your reader, you fail to grab that reader's interest in the story and its outcome. The reader simply doesn't care as much or at all.

One place where the omniscient viewpoint works well is in a family history where as the author, you can't, of course, have been on the scene with all of your family members to do the reporting of events.

The reason the omniscient viewpoint works well in fantasy, science fiction and some historical and/or epic stories is because the reader doesn't need the emotional identification with the characters like is needed in, say the literary or mainstream story or the memoir. Readers read fantasy, sci-fi, and this kind of story for other reasons such as setting and what happens in other worlds. These stories are seldom character driven.

THIRD PERSON:

The third person voice gives the reader a bit of distance from the protagonist and the other characters in the story, and gives the author the option of using dual or multiple viewpoint--in a book length work, such as a novel or family history, that is. The short story or the personal experience story, with few exceptions, always employs just one viewpoint. This is because the short fictional or personal story is focused solely on one heightened moment in one character's life, exploring that moment as fully as possible. To move into more than one character's viewpoint in the short story is to fragment the story.

Look at your story and ponder which character owns the goal and conflict and whose perspective you need for maximum suspense, for authenticity, for communicating your theme most effectively. Limit your story to as few characters as possible. Too many viewpoints can make your story feel unfocused and cluttered.

FIRST PERSON:

The first person voice is one that is up close and personal (e.g "I" felt depressed about what happened, but "I" didn't want anyone to pity "me.") This would include the memoir, of course, or any personal story you're thinking about writing. Many literary and mainstream stories are first person because they're character driven and it's important to bring the reader inside of the protagonist as deeply as possible in order to understand the motivations and deep inner workings of that character. You want to use first person when you're creating a character whom you'd like to bring into your reader's living room so that she can fully tell her story. It's usually a very personal and important story for the character and so the first person voice is really the only choice there is. Intuitively, as a writer, you know this.

There are some characters we would rather not be up close and personal with, so keep that in mind when choosing this viewpoint. Hannibal Lector or Ted Bundy would fall into this category. Hitler. People like that, real life or fictional.

If you're writing a story in the viewpoint of an outlaw/hero protagonist, or if this is your personal story and much of it is about your crime, you're going to need to help the reader empathize with your point of view. This means getting her on board and keeping her there. You do that by revealing motivation and vulnerability all along the way. What drove you to make the choices you made? Help the reader connect to and identify with you by revealing the kind of human desperation we all experience when we're down. This is not for the purpose of exploiting or manipulating the reader but for the purpose of helping her understand who you were to be able to have made the choices you made at the time.

The purpose of this course is to help you communicate a story to your reader as authentically and as clearly as possible. This is a creative process and as you can see by now, includes many components, of which the voice and viewpoint is only one. Don't worry if it hasn't all come together for you yet. The creative process can't be rushed or forced--it must be received. Let your characters talk to you and be open to the character or characters who are clamoring to be heard.

ASSIGNMENT:

1) Write a dramatic scene or a narrative summary of the hero's *Refusal of the Call.* Your hero has been called to his adventure, but he's not so keen on leaving the comforts of the *Ordinary World.* If he's going to resist, here is where to introduce his greatest fear as fear is the only reason a hero would resist the *Call.* It's not that he's a complete coward, though he could be, but more that he knows it's risky, and he's not sure he's up to the task. Include some back story if it fits to begin to fill in what his fear is all about.

Please choose one of the following options:

- *Write a short Refusal of the Call scene of 1000 or fewer words.*
- *Write one scene and a summary of the other scenes in the Refusal of the Call.*
- *Write a summary of all of the scenes in the Refusal of the Call.*

2) Create a profile for your hero in 500 or fewer words. Emphasize, not the details of his appearance but the answers to the above questions in our section on the hero. If you don't feel that you have enough words, you can create a list, if you'd like, rather than a narrative profile.

3) Choosing your story's voice/viewpoint is something that can take some time. If you're still figuring this out, and since you'll most likely use either the first- or third-person viewpoint for your story, write one 400-word scene in each, but choose a different character and/or situation for each viewpoint scene so that you're not simply exchanging one pronoun

Your Hero's Profile:

Character's Full Name:
Birthdate:
Age:
Eye Color:
Hair color and cut:
Height:
Weight:
Health:
Addiction:
Religion/religious beliefs:
Hometown:
Darkest secret:
Others' perceptions:
Occupation:
Family Relationships:
Vehicle:
Pets:
Most prized possession:
Favorite music, movie, television show:
Other pertinent information:

for another. (Omniscient isn't completely out of the question, especially if you're writing science fiction or fantasy.) If your hero is also an outlaw, reveal him in a sympathetic light.

LESSON FOUR

MEETING WITH THE MENTOR,
THE ROLE OF THE HERALD &
OUTLINING YOUR HERO'S JOURNEY STORY

A MENTOR AT A CRUCIAL POINT IN MY LIFE once gave me permission to cry anytime, anywhere. I had been "locked up" emotionally for many years, so this was good news. And that's what I've been doing ever since--crying. No, I'm not suggesting that you start crying, especially as an outlaw locked up with a bunch of other outlaws. Wouldn't be good for your image.

The point is that mentors come into our lives at strategic times and encourage and support us in ways that strengthen us along our *Hero's Journey*. Depending on the journey and the hero's need, the mentor's role can be huge. Think back. Who were your mentors? Then and now?

I've talked to a large number of prisoners who can point to several mentors they've met since they've been in prison. It seems that the mentor archetype is more alive and well in prison than just about anywhere else. It seems that the older prisoners, the ones who have been incarcerated for a while, consider it their responsibility to protect the "youngsters," the ones just entering the prison system, to teach them the ropes. It could be that you're a mentor for other inmates who are younger and more inexperienced than you.

It seems to me that without a mentor, many of us would be destined for heroless journeys. In other words, our destiny would be that of a tragic hero, because there's been no one to show us the way. This is how important the role of mentor is, and so how important it is that you carefully consider where and how the mentor(s) show up in your story.

STAGE FOUR: MEETING WITH THE MENTOR

OUR MENTORS, FOR WHATEVER REASON, take an interest in us and are in our lives to give us guidance. It might be a pastor, teacher, parent, grandparent or other person who cares about who we become as we make major decisions as in whether or not to accept a *Call to Adventure*.

Lately, I've wondered whether "outlaws" have gotten the short end of the stick when it comes to mentors. Maybe some of us are outlaws by default because of a shortage of real mentors in our lives. Or maybe you were just too angry to listen to your mentor by the time he dropped by your life. Maybe you saw him as weak rather than the mentor that he was trying to be.

In a story, the hero's relationship with his mentor is often the most meaningful relationship he has. The mentor can appear once or many times, but he usually shows up early in the story to begin to illuminate the journey for the hero. While, like the herald, the mentor can be a non-human newspaper article or a set of beliefs, I tend to think it's best if the mentor is a person so that the hero can interact with him along the way. And while the mentor may offer external gifts to the hero, his influence is often an internal one as his wisdom can raise a hero's consciousness or challenge him to new heights he didn't know he was capable of accomplishing.

The mentor is often the character who delivers the story's theme to the reader because he's a little wiser than the hero and can often see what the journey is about for the hero before he can see it for himself. So, when the two of them are in conversation about the meaning of the journey, the mentor is often the one who articulates that meaning when the hero is still struggling.

It does happen sometimes that the mentor is a dark character who doesn't necessarily have the best interest of the hero at heart. Or he could be a well-meaning character who, even though he only wants to help, is a wounded hero himself. He may disappoint or become obsessed with the hero. He could even be a shadow or a shapeshifter, which can put an interesting spin on a story. This is a dark mentor, an outlaw in his own right.

Think through your hero's first meeting with the mentor. What happens?

Who is the source of wisdom the hero turns to before saying "yes" to the journey?

How does the mentor come alongside the hero to guide and equip him for the journey?

Is the mentor an outlaw, and does he or she become obsessed, deceive or mislead the hero in any way? If so, how?

When does the Meeting with the Mentor occur in the story? How does the mentor help the hero get across the first threshold?

THE ROLE OF THE HERALD

Herald energy:
• awareness of good/bad news without a vested interest in the outcome

• shaking of one's world

• positive, negative, or neutral

• attention-getting

• provides new opportunities

• strong pull on emotions, psyche, spirit

• feeling of restlessness

• an anxiety attack

THE HERALD USUALLY APPEARS AT THE END of the opening scene, at the point of *The Call to Adventure* to present the journey to the hero. Like the mentor, he doesn't absolutely have to be a human being—he could be an idea, a figure in a dream, a new piece of information (like something the hero might hear on television or read on the Internet), but again, I tend to think it's best if he's a human being so that the hero has another character with whom to interact when he's presented with the invitation to move into the special world.

The herald can present both an external special world and an internal world of transformation, preferably both. His role includes provoking the hero into action, and so providing motivation for the journey. He can be a "good" guy or a "bad" guy or neutral. Who the herald is isn't as important as the function he fulfills in the hero's story—he's the catalyst that propels the hero on his journey. In your journey to prison, as mentioned in an earlier chapter, the herald may have been the arresting officer, the prosecutor, or the judge. In *Man On Wire,* the true story of Phillipe Petit who, on August 7, 1974, strung a cable from one of New York's still-standing twin towers to the other and walked across eight times, the herald was a newspaper article Petit came across in a dentist's office when the twin towers were just an idea in someone's mind. He ripped the article out of the newspaper, knowing that he would conquer those towers. And he did.

As an outlaw, if you're writing a personal story, you might want to think about that pivotal moment where you crossed the line into lawlessness. Or maybe you would consider yourself an accidental outlaw. Maybe you are in prison but are innocent of the crime for which you were convicted—there was still a pivotal moment where a herald appeared and presented you with the opportunity to go on the journey through the justice system that led you to prison. You may curse that day, you may curse the herald and his announcement, but you're here, and the *Hero's Journey* can help you make sense of this life situation in which you find yourself.

Once the herald announces the journey, the hero must respond, agreeing or refusing the journey before him. Up until this time, the hero has just been getting by. Not happy. Not fulfilled.

Who fulfills the role of the herald archetype in your story?

Is the herald a human being and how does he make his approach?

What does the herald present to the hero that provokes him to agree to the journey?

Herald's purpose:
External:
• kicks off the plot/ initiates the journey

• issues the *Call to Adventure*

• gets the hero's attention/wakes him up just a bit

• tells the hero he has a job to do

• speaks louder than anything else going on in the hero's world

• carries the message of the power of destiny

• brings awareness of impending danger

OUTLINING YOUR HERO'S JOURNEY STORY

MANY MEMOIR AND NOVEL WRITERS I'VE WORKED WITH over the years have balked at the idea of outlining before they write their story. Writers of how-to, self-help, business, and other kinds of non-fiction books understand that it's part of the preparation process in writing a book. But many writers of stories perceive the outline as putting a limit on their creativity. I understand this, especially for literary writers whose focus is more on character development than it is on plot and action.

So, in order to work with *The Hero's Journey*, how do we get past our judgments and aversions to outlining? The answer to this question is that we begin to see the value of the outline, which for the sake of working with *The Hero's Journey*, we can call form or structure or system. We don't have to use the word, outline. It's true that outlining, while not easy, is less challenging for a genre story with the focus more on what happens than for a literary or mainstream story with the focus more on how what happens affects the characters' internal transformations. But the major weakness of the literary or mainstream story is that not enough happens for the characters to respond to, while the major weakness of the genre story is that what happens doesn't make a lot of difference in who the characters become. The value of *The Hero's Journey* is that, if understood, it can facilitate both the external and the internal journey of the hero so that you end up with a story that truly connects with readers because it includes both 1) action that moves the story events and pleases genre readers and 2) the transformation of character that gives each story its meaning and so satisfies literary and mainstream readers.

You may just be starting to write a memoir or novel. You may be halfway through writing the first draft. You may have written the first draft and are on now in the revision process. At whatever stage, you bring in *The Hero's Journey*, you will benefit greatly from understanding that whether or not we're conscious of it, our lives and stories fall into a natural order

Herald's purpose:
Internal:

• .provokes the inner realization that something needs to change, that life can't go on the way it has

• appears as a dream, vision, still small voice of the Divine

• provides the hero with motivation

• alerts the hero to something he can no longer tolerate

• challenges the hero to do something greater than he's ever done, to be something greater than he's ever been

when we're moving from initial conflict to resolution of that conflict and the subsequent insight. This natural order is *The Hero's Journey*, and once you learn how this powerful system works in ordering our stories, you'll probably never go back to the haphazard way you were previously trying to structure your stories, if indeed, you thought about structure at all.

By now you probably understand that *The Hero's Journey* has two primary elements with which you want to familiarize yourself; a list of archetypes and the stages of the journey. You've mused over a few ideas and come up with one, hopefully, that you feel passionately about and confident that you can turn into a story. Okay, even if the confidence isn't there, the potential is.

Now stories consist of many elements; characters, structure, theme, viewpoint, setting, pacing, dialogue, action, etc. The element we're going to focus on in this lecture is structure. Without a structure, your story won't hold together. Without a structure, your story will bend and twist for no particular reason and eventually collapse somewhere in the middle. Without a structure, your story will meander all over the place and end up communicating a fuzzy message to the reader, if it communicates one at all. But with a solid structure, you will create a flow for your story that will carry your story's characters and readers on a smooth ride from beginning to end, and clearly communicate the story's truth.

Famous Heralds:
John the Baptist
The town crier
Michael Moore
Bob Dylan/Joan Baez
Rolling Stone Magazine

When pondering the structure of your story, the first thing you can do to prepare to write is to create an outline, which you'll be able to use as a guide to move you and your characters from the story's beginning to the story's end.

Above we mentioned how abhorrent the outline is to some writers—as abhorrent as Brussels sprouts are to some children. But I'm not just a writer, I'm a writing coach, and writing coaches understand the value of outlining—because we know how uncomfortable it is for, especially new writers, to get stuck in the middle of a story, not know where they're going, and get frustrated, eventually giving up altogether on the story.

Some stories are easier to outline than others. When outlining plot-driven fictional stories, you simply have to think through a number of plot events to oppose your character as he pursues his goal. Or if you're writing a personal plot-driven story, say, a dramatic personal experience like encountering a cougar in the woods or a near drowning incident, again, your outline will consist of one obstacle after the other working against your survival.

If you're writing a character-driven story, though, say, a literary story of any kind or any story where you or a character of your imagination is transformed by the story events, outlining is more difficult. This is because a character's internal growth, better known in storytelling as his character arc, is more difficult to measure than the external events that lead to that growth.

There are many kinds of outlines, and you have to find the one that works best for you. Some writers just create a brief narrative passage for each scene or chapter. Some outline all of the action and dialogue in each scene. Some simply create a narrative synopsis of the entire story. If you're new at outlining, it would be good for you to think through your story outline in some detail, deciding on your 1) dramatic scenes and 2) reflective sequels as your pivotal points.

"Heralds have the important psychological function of announcing the need for change. Something deep inside us knows when we are ready to change and sends us a messenger."
~ Chris Vogler

Ordering the Stages and Archetypes into a Form

YOU DON'T ABSOLUTELY HAVE TO CREATE an entire outline before you write your story. You could create it as you write. It's just that doing the work ahead of time will assure a smoother ride than if you head into the story, trying to then make the outline fit the story you want to write. It's kind of like laying the foundation of the house before you start erecting the walls and putting the roof on. There are just some things that come first.

Each of your characters has one primary role, but these can shift around. Your antagonist might primarily play the role of the shadow, but at times he might shift into a mentor or a trickster. Think through your cast of characters so that you know each character's major role. The story revolves around your hero, and each other character in the story either opposes him or supports him. It's as simple as that.

Consider your hero's entire journey, the ups and downs of the plot, the emotional highs and lows the character experiences as he moves from one stage to the next. Plan a series of big scenes for him at each stage and more subtle moments in between where he steps back to reflect. Ponder where he needs to meet other characters and how they will help move him forward or set him back. His internal development as a character should parallel the external movement of the story.

What I love about *The Hero's Journey* is that it gives us a template for our plots. We can be as creative as we want to be in creating scenes, in how we get our hero from one point to the next, but in case we start to get lost, we always have a map in *The Hero's Journey* to bring us back to what the story is really all about for our hero.

If this is your first time working with *The Hero's Journey*, you may find it a challenging ride, well, just like the first time you rode a roller coaster. You don't know what to expect. The second time you know a little more about what to expect, although each new story brings its unique challenges. As you get used to using *The Hero's Journey* template for your stories, the ride is no less exhilarating, but it is less scary. So hang on for the ride. You'll reap a big reward at the end, just like your hero.

Crafting scenes

EVERY STORY IS, OR SHOULD BE, CREATED SCENE BY SCENE. Like a child building a tower of blocks, scenes are built one upon another. Thaisa Frank and Dorothy Wall (*Finding your Writer's Voice*) give us another way to look at creating a plot or story line: "You understand instinctively that a good plot functions like a series of billiard balls hitting against each other." It's cause and effect; every scene causes an effect that leads into the next scene that causes another effect and so on. In between the dramatic scenes we need sequels to give the reader a moment to breathe and so that the main character can catch up with himself. If you're writing about your own life, these are the moments you punch a wall (hopefully not a fellow inmate or a guard), walk the yard, throw something, and figure out what you're going to do next. More about sequels below.

Every dramatic scene should have three elements. Jack Bickham, in his excellent book, *Scene & Structure*, calls these elements goal, conflict and disaster. I call them intention, journey and collision. If you're writing a personal story, you want to identify your intention or goal right away so that the reader can get on board and so that the story begins to propel forward. The best way to reveal your goal is through a scene of dialogue and action that *shows* rather than through a few narrative paragraphs that *tell*. Knowing your intention is what causes the story to begin to move for the reader—there's something you're reaching for and the story events will engage the reader as the obstacles begin to show up and you fail time and time again to reach your goal.

The series of obstacles is the journey part of the story and reveals your external and internal conflict, whatever it is. It could be that you're running a race and your goal is the finish line—that's external. But the internal goal could be much deeper—you want to prove to yourself that you can finish what you start which is something you've never been able to do before.

If you're writing fiction, it's the same process. Your protagonist has a goal, but is faced with a conflict that grows more and more intense as the scene progresses. Finally, at the end of the scene, your hero collides—with another character, with a physical obstacle, with his own value system. And he's temporarily derailed. The goal/intention can come from within or without, preferably both. The journey/conflict can also come from within or without. And the collision can be a physical one coming from something external, or it can be emotional, psychological, or spiritual and come from within. The best stories are ones that occur in both the external and internal dimensions.

At the point of impact—collision—the character can then slide into a sequel, which will give both character and reader a moment to catch a breath before the next scene begins.

Crafting scene sequels

IN REAL LIFE, WE REACT TO DRAMATIC EVENTS, and so, in a story, you want to give your character a chance to react, whether the character is you or is fictional. Sequels are important components of any story because they twist and turn the story and take it in a certain direction determined by the character's reaction.

Just as a scene needs the three elements of intention, journey and collision, the sequel also needs certain elements in order to effectively communicate the character's reaction. These elements are: emotion, thought, decision, and action.

You or your character react to what just happened in the previous dramatic scene with some emotion; sorrow, anger, terror, joy, frustration, nervousness—there are a myriad of types and intensity of emotions. While our hero is processing the emotion, he's starting to think about what he needs to do to get out of the pain, to fix the problem, whatever it is. The emotion and thought part of the sequel often take place simultaneously or shift back and forth throughout the sequel.

The decision part of the sequel is what drives the sequel. By this, I mean that the hero's need to make a decision should be paramount. The story's plot should be twisting and turning as it moves, and every time the hero makes a decision, that's exactly what starts to happen. The hero is responsible for shifting the story line in the sequel so that it moves in a slightly different or very different direction. The pressure to make this decision can cause the hero much stress and give the sequel needed tension and suspense.

The action part of the sequel can occur right after the decision or even later in the next chapter or scene or several scenes later. The hero makes the decision which leads to action which twists the story line and moves it forward. If your story is strongly character driven, the hero's decisions will usually create some kind of internal transformation. This is how you show who the hero is becoming as the story events unfold; how he reacts to the dramatic events in his life and the kinds of decisions he makes as a result.

While we can't be exhaustive here in our discussion of scenes and sequels, you should now have a pretty good handle on how to construct a plot or story line for your factual or fictional story. These are the elements that will engage the reader in your story and keep it moving forward, so we can never underestimate their importance. Everything else in your story hinges on how well you develop your scenes and sequels.

ASSIGNMENT:

Write a dramatic 1000-word (or fewer) scene or a narrative summary of your hero's *Meeting with the Mentor*. This is the point in the story where the hero receives wisdom from a wiser being, a character who has some experience with the journey on which your hero is about to embark. The mentor can be an intangible; a book, a quote, a song, something that begins to impart wisdom and direct the hero's life in a way he hadn't anticipated. But preferably this should be another character; it can be a homeless person, a child (children are sometimes old souls in the way they look at the world), or a mentally handicapped individual. What makes for an effective mentor in a story is the degree of wisdom the individual possesses and your protagonist's ability to recognize the mentor archetype and what this character is making available to him.

1) Please choose one of the following options:

- Write a short *Meeting with the Mentor* scene of 1000 words
- Write one scene and a summary of the other scenes in the *Meeting with the Mentor*
- Write a summary of all of the scenes in the *Meeting with the Mentor* stage

2) Create a profile for your herald in 300 or fewer words. Emphasize, not the details of his appearance but the answers to the above questions in our section on the herald. Focus specifically on his role in *The Hero's Journey*.

Who is this character and how does he introduce the *Call to Adventure* to the hero?

3) Create an outline in 500 or fewer words that shows the positioning of your scenes and sequels. If you can't include everything in 500 words (say, if you're writing a novel with a complex plot), then just get started, planning the first few scenes and sequels, or write a detailed narrative synopsis that includes the most pivotal scenes leading up to the crisis, climax, and insight that signals the end of *The Hero's Journey*.

LESSON FIVE

CROSSING THE FIRST THRESHOLD, THE ROLE OF THE MENTOR & CHOOSING YOUR STORY'S SETTING

As an outlaw who's been arrested, the arrest is your *Call to Adventure*. To cross the first threshold could be that first step into jail or prison or into a courtroom. It's different for each person. *Crossing the First Threshold*, while an external act, is also an internal agreement with yourself to move ahead into the special world. You may have agreed to go on the journey, which is what the *Call to Adventure* and the *Refusal of the Call* is all about. But you may not have a clue as to what you've just agreed to. So when you approach the threshold, another agreement is necessary. A contract, if you will.

The hero makes a contract with himself to cross the threshold and trust that he'll be able to conquer whatever challenges he encounters in the special world. This is not something he's always conscious he's doing. It's often instinctual, not something thought out. If it was thought out, if he even considered what might be ahead, he might never make the crossing in the first place. Because, like it or not, whether we admit it or not, and as an outlaw/hero, you're going to hate me pointing this out, but inside every big boy is a scared little boy, just like within every big girl is a scared little girl. At the *Crossing of the First Threshold*, that scared little boy is going to rise up and fill the hero with self-doubt that he's strong enough to make the journey.

Crossing the First Threshold is about finding that strong place inside of yourself, that place that feels like granite, where you know there is no turning back.

STAGE FIVE: CROSSING THE FIRST THRESHOLD

THE HERO'S FIRST THRESHOLD CAN BE PHYSICAL, emotional, intellectual, or psychological. This is the moment where the hero has a decision to make—will he go on the journey or won't he? Even if a character is forced into a physical journey (kidnapping, physical and possibly fatal disease, a move across the country), he can hold back from crossing the emotional, intellectual, and psychological threshold. For example, when you were arrested, you may have physically resisted, making it worse for yourself, of course. (I remember a time my son resisted arrest, which ended with the cops beating the crap out of him and dropping him off at the hospital before they returned to take him to jail. I think I can safely say that he would have preferred avoiding the side trip to the hospital.) Your hero may not be able to do anything about the physical journey he is being forced into, but only when he decides to take the internal journey, does he fully cross the first threshold, agreeing, howbeit grudgingly, to go on the journey. Even when other characters are coming against our hero, even if he's an outlaw, he has the freedom to choose what he's going to do and how he's going to internally react. You must know your hero well in order to know what he'll do.

As an outlaw, a hero may resist just because that's what he does. He won't go on a journey just because conventional wisdom, those in his *Ordinary World*, or his family or mentors think he should. The outlaw always questions, always challenges—that's partly what makes him an outlaw. If he has the chance to think about it, he'll probably always resist—unless the journey itself is anti-society, anti-conventional, anti-authority. Then he'll go quite willingly, often because no one else thinks he should. Part of the internal journey of the outlaw is to learn that going on a *Hero's Journey* should be determined by what his gut instincts are telling him as he moves toward love rather than fear, not whether or not society sanctions the journey.

It should come as no surprise to you that threshold guardians show up at the first threshold. It's up to the hero to be creative and find a way around them IF he's committed to the journey. The threshold guardians aren't always real—they might be illusions in the hero's mind; still, they're real to him, and so must be overcome.

Sometimes a hero will find some kind of symbol or prop that marks the crossing between the ordinary and special world. What physical item did you have to give up when you went to prison, an item that meant everything to you? The crossing could be marked by a literal navigational device such as a bridge or river or road.

According to Chris Vogler, sometimes the hero has to muster up his courage and faith at the first threshold and make a leap out of the *Ordinary World*—this could mean a literal or physical crashing into the special world.

Consider the catalyst for your hero—what will launch him into his journey? However he gets there, this is his first big step, so as storyteller, make it a memorable one.

What is the catalyst that launches your hero into his journey? Does he resist or go willingly? If he resists, it could be the outlaw in him rising up—what is his attitude about the journey that causes his resistance?

What does the threshold guardian do at the threshold to prevent the hero from making his crossing?

What is the symbol or prop that marks the hero's crossing?

What does your hero do to bypass or conquer each threshold guardian?

What is your hero's moment of faith that helps him get across? Does he cross gently or does he crash into the special world?

THE ROLE OF THE MENTOR

A MENTOR IS USUALLY, BUT NOT ALWAYS, a support character for the hero. He might train him, cheer him or protect him, but he most certainly imparts to the hero the wisdom he needs for the journey. The mentor speaks and acts from a place of wisdom and spiritual insight. Mentor energy in the story equals the hero's highest self, his conscience; it might remind him of his personal value system.

The mentor often comes into the story bearing gifts for the hero. These gifts can be external and tangible—a key, a light, a weapon for the journey. Or the gift can be intangible—a warning, a challenge, a revelation, some piece of advice or inspiration. The mentor doesn't just hand the gift over to the hero; the hero earns it in some way. As discussed above, he may have to sacrifice something that meant everything to him in *The Ordinary World*. The mentor may want the hero to pass one or a series of tests before he deems him worthy of the gift.

The mentor motivates the hero, supports him and helps him overcome his fear and reluctance to go on the journey. Sometimes he does this by planting a bit of information or a tangible prop of some kind that the hero will later remember and use to save his life.

Some mentors are just friends on the journey—others are spiritual teachers whose function is to coach your hero in his life quest. Some are human beings; some are intangible--a code of ethics, a set of principles that informs the hero's behavior and guides his important decisions.

As we talked about in our last lesson, sometimes the mentor is a shadow figure, a dark character, an outlaw himself who is wounded and hasn't yet healed his wound. He may be a tragic hero. Still, he has learned some things, even if he hasn't yet applied them. The hero can encounter more than one mentor in a story. If the mentor is an outlaw, it may be that as the hero begins to transform himself, he knows he can no longer listen to

Mentor energy:

• the higher self; wiser, nobler, more godlike part of us

• a protective spirit

• the motivation and inspiration to keep going

• can be an intangible; a disembodied manifestation guiding the hero's actions

• an internalized code of behavior or ethics or piece of advice

the tragic-hero mentor and must move away from him in order to keep growing as a person. He may encounter another mentor who is walking in more light. Be aware of your hero's character arc as he interacts with all of the other characters. How he interacts, how he perceives them, is what begins to reveal his arc, how he's changing on the inside.

Oftentimes, it's the mentor who conveys the story's theme to both the hero and the reader. The hero must experience and learn the truth the journey is trying to teach him, but because the mentor is a little ahead of the hero, he often sees the truth first and may point it out.

Every story needs a mentor as every hero learns from someone who has preceded him on the journey,

Who is the mentor in your story? Is there more than one?

What does the mentor teach your hero? What does he give him?

Is the mentor a tragic hero and does he lead the hero down a path that isn't in his best interest? How will you show this?

How does the hero earn the gift from his mentor?

Does the mentor plant a piece of information or a prop? What?

Does the mentor point out the story's theme to the hero? When and where?

Mentor's purpose:
Internal:
• to act as a conscience for the hero
• to pass on gifts of knowledge and wisdom
• to motivate, drive, and help the hero overcome fear
• to initiate the hero into the mysteries of love and/or sex
• to provide emotional support
• to serve as a shaman; a force to help the hero seek a guiding vision for a quest to another world
• to strengthens the hero's mind to face an ordeal with confidence

CHOOSING YOUR STORY'S SETTING

YOUR STORY MAY HAVE MORE THAN ONE SETTING. It probably does. But there's usually one major pervasive setting. Whether writing a story from your own life or a fictional story, you want to set it somewhere that's intriguing and enhances the story in some way. Also, when considering your setting, think as broadly as you can. The setting isn't just the room in which the journey takes place. It's not just the geographical location of your memoir or novel. It's not just a building or a locale, though it can be that. But it can also be much more.

A setting can be an entire industry or culture. It can be the red light district in LA or the music industry in Nashville. It can be a physical building in Detroit, or it can encompass an entire village and tribe in Africa. It can be a physical church building or it can be a religion in which the hero is raised. The story's setting is all of the physical and emotional details surrounding your character and can either be a backdrop for the story or can be a character or archetype itself with a negative or positive effect on your life, if a personal story, or your hero's life, if fiction.

If you want your reader to get the full effect of your setting on your hero, you'll need to use as many sensory details as possible. Create smells, sights, sounds, tastes, and aesthetic moments that will draw your reader into the story at a sensory level. This is one way you engage your reader in the story. Not just a sweet smell, but a smell of roses and honeysuckle. Not just a bitter taste, but the taste of cold lemons.

A fully developed setting can make the reader believe that your story is really happening. As a writing coach, when I read a story where the writer has failed to develop the setting, the story feels as though it's taking place in a vacuum, as if the characters are talking heads in outer space somewhere. If you think it doesn't matter, that your story could take place just anywhere, then you don't yet know what your story is really all about. How you or your characters interact with the setting can tell us a lot about who you or your characters are, how you or your characters perceive the world, what you or your characters value. It's that important.

Mentor's purpose:
External:

• to model what the hero may become if he stays on the journey

• to teach, train, and guide the hero as he moves through the stages

• to give tangible gifts that help the hero navigate the journey (must earn these gifts)

• to push the reluctant hero

• to plant information that will become important later in the story

• to show up at just the right time when the hero is ready

• to understand the hero's past fear and send him on to the brink of adventure

ASSIGNMENT:

Write a dramatic scene or a narrative summary of your hero's *Crossing the First Threshold,* where he will be tested and encounter his allies and enemies (the stage to come). Will he cross readily, or does his outlaw self rise up? Will he be forced across? Who are the threshold guardians he will meet there? What will it take to get him to make the crossing? Is there a symbol or prop to mark the crossing?

1) Please choose one of the following options:

• Write a short *Crossing the First Threshold* scene of 1000 words

• Write one scene and a summary of the other scenes in the *Crossing the First Threshold*

• Write a summary of all of the scenes in the *Crossing the First Threshold* stage

2) Create a profile for your mentor in 300 or fewer words. Emphasize, not the details of his appearance, but the answers to the above questions in our section on the mentor. Focus specifically on his role in *The Hero's Journey.* Who is this character? What is the wisdom he imparts to the hero, and how does he impart it?

3) Write a 250-word scene that reveals your story's major setting. Use sensory details to show your hero interacting with the setting and so bring it to life for the reader.

LESSON SIX

TESTS, ALLIES & ENEMIES,
THE ROLE OF THE THRESHOLD GUARDIAN
& CRAFTING DIALOGUE THAT DELIVERS

I STARTED VOLUNTEERING IN A MEN'S PRISON near my home over 15 years ago now. At the time, I had no idea I was embarking on a *Hero's Journey*. No one close into my life ever asked me what I was doing up there, and when I mentioned it, the conversation would suddenly thud. No questions. No comments. Just nothing. I longed to talk about it, mostly what I was learning about myself in doing this. I'd started volunteering simply because I was writing a novel, and one of my characters was on death row. I had a few questions, and the prison was running a 7-week class for the community. After the class was over, I stayed on as a volunteer as something, I wasn't sure what at the time, was deeply resonating for me.

It was only when I decided to stay in touch with some of the men after they were released, forming friendships with a few of them, that I started having a bit of a conflict in some of my personal relationships. My friends didn't understand where I was coming from in doing this. I have to say that most of my friends and family accepted my decision, but I remember, in particular, one friend who couldn't tolerate it.

"I don't understand why you would welcome into your life men who have abused women and children," were her words to me. And then she was gone. After 15 years of close friendship, we never spoke again. I wanted to tell her that if these men, newly released from prison, were currently abusing women and children, while I would try my best to love them from afar, they wouldn't be close into my life. But I knew that wouldn't be enough for her. She just didn't feel safe in my life any more with these men around. And so I let her go. Not an "enemy" certainly, but no longer a friend.

It's true that we're tested on the journey, and the people in our lives begin to separate into two camps. I watch this happen all of the time—in my own life and in the lives of those I love. When you were sentenced to prison, I'm guessing that you may have lost a few people in the process. Those who, once they saw you convicted of a crime, once there was no more doubt in their minds that you were, indeed, a criminal, wanted no more to do with you. It does seem that families stick by more than friends, but sometimes even family members leave us at this part of the journey.

TESTS, ALLIES, AND ENEMIES

THIS STAGE IS THE FULL ENTRANCE INTO THE HERO'S SPECIAL WORLD which should be in sharp contrast to the *Ordinary World*. In the special world, the hero has a new mission with new challenges, different goals, and unexpected encounters with allies and enemies that require more of him than was required in the *Ordinary World*. He will now be tested in ways he's never been tested before.

The hero gathers his allies as he's able to determine who's on his side and who's most likely to stay on his side, who he needs and who he doesn't, who believes in him and who doesn't, who respects him and who doesn't. (Outlaws, as I'm sure you know, are big on respect.) Allies may travel part of the way with the hero, then split off onto a different path, or the whole way. The ally/sidekick may provide comic relief on the journey, as heroes can sometimes take themselves too seriously.

The testing is not usually something the hero is familiar with, and so he's forced to exercise muscles he hasn't previously exercised. This can cause him to feel like a failure at first, like he's not cut out for whatever is before him. He will have to dig deep inside of himself for the resources he needs to conquer his own internal demons as well as the enemies he finds outside of himself. He's confronted with new rules in the special world, ones he may at first resist. He also may refuse to see their necessity. Will your hero be able to adjust to the conditions of his new environment?

The dark side of the outlaw often perceives his allies as his enemies and his enemies as his allies. This is partly what makes him an outlaw—while he may perceive himself as strong, in another sense, he's weak because his antenna isn't always up as to who's supporting him and who's out to get him. He often doesn't have good boundaries, and when the tests come along, he often blows them off as just so much BS. Then he gets confused when he feels betrayed by his friends, and he begins to see himself as a victim. The outlaw begins to distrust everyone and their motives, when what he needs is to trust himself and his own instincts.

In this world, group experiences are often useful in order for your hero to meet new people and begin to sort out his allies and enemies. Chris Vogler calls the places where your hero has his group experiences, "watering holes," but when thinking about contemporary stories, what are the meeting places of today's special world? Bars? Internet cafes? Twelve-step groups? Be creative so that your meeting place is more than just a cliché. In prison, one meeting place might be the yard. Are there other places where the inmates are free to hang out? The gym, the weight room, a television room?

As the hero begins to discern who's for and who's against him, special sojourners will begin to emerge—both negative and positive. If you haven't already, you could begin to introduce the shadow character and/or the hero's best buddy at this stage. These characters don't have to be new friends—they may have been around for a long time, but in the special world, they emerge as stronger in influence than before. They may even switch roles from who they were in the *Ordinary World*.

How will you reveal the differences between the Ordinary World and the special world?

Who are your hero's enemies and how do they become enemies? Are they connected to the shadow/antagonist and if so, how?

How is your hero able to sort out his enemies from his allies?

What are the new rules of the special world, and is the hero up to adhering to them?

What is your hero's meeting place in the special world?

Threshold Guardian's purpose:
Internal:
• to torment the hero with internal demons, neuroses, emotional scars, vices, dependencies and self-limitations that hold him back from growth and progress

• to surface painful memories that paralyze and prevent the hero from moving forward

• to demonstrate the hero's major weakness early on in the story

• to serve as a minor reflection of what the hero will face in the shadow character

THE ROLE OF THE THRESHOLD GUARDIAN

THE ROLE OF THE THRESHOLD GUARDIAN is to test your hero whenever he's preparing to take the next step of the journey. It's his job to prevent the (in his mind) unworthy and undeserving hero from entering the new worlds along the journey. This is an important role as it holds your hero accountable for his personal growth so as to be able to enter the next stage.

To the outlaw/hero, a threshold guardian can look like an enemy, like he's against the hero. This may or may not be true. When the dark side of the hero is active, he's usually not open to anyone's influence, and a threshold guardian's appearance may only enrage him. The threshold guardian may be a caring presence, wanting only the best for the outlaw, but the outlaw probably won't see it that way, not at first.

If our outlaw/hero is willing to invest the time and energy to try to understand the threshold guardian, this archetype can often be conquered, bypassed or turned into an ally. The hero can't let himself be put off by a seemingly impossible-to-get-around threshold guardian. The brave hero sees this archetype-character as a challenge, even if he's not conscious of exactly what the challenge is. Parents are often the kinds of threshold guardians the hero may at first try to bypass, then turn into an ally. When a parent comes against us, we just don't often see at first that that person could really be for us, even if he or she is against what we're doing at the moment.

Threshold guardians who are also outlaws are often in some way connected to the antagonist—working for him, a friend of his with a similar agenda for the hero. He or she will often try to get the hero to rethink whether it's a worthwhile goal to stay on the journey. He may tell him that his goal/objective is beyond his reach, that he's not up to the task of succeeding in his pursuit. He may herald an escalation of the danger the hero faces, reminding the hero that the journey is an arduous one, not worth the trouble.

The internal energy of the threshold guardian torments the hero by surfacing his outlaw archetype's demons, neuroses, emotional scars, vices, addictions and self-limitations that hold him back on the path. Painful memories might surface that paralyze and prevent the hero from moving forward.

One way for your hero to deal with a threshold guardian is to get inside of him, to learn how he thinks. So these archetypes are sometimes not defeated but incorporated. The hero may absorb the threshold guardian's tactics and then move on.

Who are the threshold guardians in your story? Are any of them outlaws?

What is your threshold guardian's view of the story situation?

What is your threshold guardian's role in blocking your hero as he pursues his goal?

What is your threshold guardian's personal agenda? If outlaws, how is that agenda "out of bounds" in a civilized society?

Is your threshold guardian for or against your hero? How so?

Threshold Guardian's purpose:
External:
• to guard access to the cave, headquarters, palace

• to try to get the hero to rethink whether or not he wishes to proceed on the journey

• to try to convince the hero that his objective/goal is beyond his reach

• to test the hero to ensure his worthiness to pass into the next phase of the journey

• to test the hero's resolve--is he serious about the journey?

• to herald an escalation of the danger the hero faces

• to reveal that the journey will be an arduous one

• to show up as ally of the shadow

CRAFTING DIALOGUE THAT DELIVERS

Threshold Guardian energy:

• shows up as an often illusory challenge

• reveals passive and/ or passive/aggressive resistance

• hinders reaching one's full potential

• resists change

• neutralizes--neither supporting nor opposing

• presents as rule keeping/policing

Famous Threshold Guardians:
Simon Cowell

Lucy (Peanuts cartoon)

Police

Teachers and principals

Parents

Judges

"At each gateway to a new world there are powerful guardians at the threshold, placed to keep the unworthy from entering."
~Chris Vogler

DIALOGUE IS MY FAVORITE TOOL for bringing characters to life on the page. Whenever a character speaks, the reader tends to listen, well, unless he's the kind of character who rambles on and on about inconsequential things. And this is the power of dialogue. Dean Koontz, the horror writer, in his book, *How to Write Best Selling Fiction*, says: "Many new writers think – erroneously – that fiction should be a mirror of reality. Actually, it should act as a sifter to *refine* reality until only the essence is before the reader. This is nowhere more evident than in fictional dialogue." I completely agree, and I think it's also true of the dialogue in our true personal stories. It's up to you to shape and sculpt and bring only the essence of your real people's dialogue before the reader.

Some writers have a fear of dialogue. They want their characters to sound profound and deep when they talk and they're afraid they won't. These writers are afraid the mystery of any character will be dispelled once he opens his mouth. They're afraid all of the dialogue in their stories will sound the same, no matter who's speaking. The only way to deal with the fear of writing dialogue is to just start writing it, reading it out loud, and getting feedback whenever you can. And the way to make sure it's authentic is to get to know your characters as well as you can so that when they speak, the dialogue that rises up from within them is organic, the part of you that is inside of them.

Dialogue serves many purposes: It can advance the story's action, reveal the characters, set the story's mood, intensify the character's conflict, succinctly convey background information to the reader, bring immediacy to the story's action, provide a change of pace in the story, create suspense, and keep the reader informed about the story movement. You don't ever want to create dialogue that doesn't perform at least some, and hopefully many, of these functions. Perfunctory dialogue is boring in real life and is boring to read; as a storyteller, you can never afford to be boring.

I've only scratched the surface on this subject. And so how can I possibly end a discussion of dialogue without mentioning my book, *Dialogue*, published by Writer's Digest Books? Of course, it's the best book out there on dialogue and comes highly recommended by the author.

ASSIGNMENT:

Write a dramatic scene or a narrative summary of your hero's *Tests, Allies & Enemies*. What is the test facing your hero that includes both new allies and/or enemies, or shows the shifting of allies to enemies or enemies to allies? (It's best if the hero's test is both external and internal.) Does he shine or does he fail miserably? What is the watering hole in the hero's new world? How is the special world different from the *Ordinary World*? What is the conflict that helps your hero distinguish between his allies and enemies?

1) Please choose one of the following options:

- Write a short *Tests, Allies & Enemies* scene of 1000 or fewer words

- Write one scene and a summary of the other scenes in *Tests, Allies & Enemies*

- Write a summary of all of the scenes in the *Tests, Allies & Enemies* stage of the journey

2) Create a profile for your threshold guardian in 300 or fewer words. Emphasize, not the details of his appearance, but the answers to the above questions in our section on the *Threshold Guardian*. Focus specifically on his role in *The Hero's Journey*. Who is this character and how does he try to prevent the hero from moving forward on the journey?

3) Write a 500-word scene of conflict, using dialogue, between your hero and the threshold guardian. This doesn't have to be a full-out argument, but there needs to be tension, and something must be at stake for the hero if the threshold guardian wins. Work at bringing out the outlaw perspective in either character's dialogue.

LESSON SEVEN

APPROACH TO THE INMOST CAVE, THE ROLE OF THE SHADOW & BUSTING THE MYTH OF "WRITER'S BLOCK"

ONCE THE HERO HAS BEEN TESTED and has sorted out his allies and enemies, he's ready for *The Approach to the Inmost Cave*. I remember a friend of mine, newly released from prison, who was hit on all sides once he got out. Even though he had worked on himself in prison and was a new man when he got out, his "victim" learned of his release and began a smear campaign on the Internet. He was preparing to be married, and her strategy to destroy him was working as his fiancé's family started freaking out, causing them to decide to postpone their wedding.

I wondered how Mark would handle this. I watched him face all kinds of tests and begin to sort through his allies and enemies. I waited for him to crumble under the stress. He had some tough days, but he hung in there, and when it came time for his *Approach* (I saw this as his day in court), he held his head high, and the judge ruled in his favor, smacking the woman with a restraining order—physically and virally. No posters on telephone poles. No internet postings or she would be in contempt of court.

We knew this wasn't the end of his *Hero's Journey*—this woman was too determined for that. But personally, I believe things started to go his way because he truly was on a *Hero's Journey*, and as long as he chose to take the high road, his integrity would continue to work in his favor.

It's scary to approach the cave as you just don't know the sizes and shapes of dragons that are in there waiting for you.

THE APPROACH TO THE INMOST CAVE

THIS IS PRETTY MUCH THE POINT OF NO RETURN FOR THE HERO. The *Inmost Cave* and the *Ordeal* within is the place where the hero will be severely tested, where secrets will be revealed, sacrifices will be made, and endurance rewarded. Stealth is required for this part of the journey; bumbling heroes won't make it through.

The hero may or may not be aware of the *Ordeal* facing him, but whether he is or not, the *Approach* is a time for preparation--it's Boot Camp for heroes. This is where the hero may begin to have a stronger sense of who he is and what his journey is all about. He's nearing the gates deep inside of the special world, and it's going to take a special strategy to navigate this part of the journey. He plans, schemes, considers where his enemies are (including the ones inside of him), holds his allies close to him and lets the others go, strengthens his inner core for what at some level, he knows is up ahead.

The *Approach* is where the outlaw/hero often messes up because he can tend to be a little impulsive. One reason outlaws end up as prisoners rather than presidents of companies (although to end up as president of a company is not out of the question; Sonny Barger, founder of The Hell's Angels, was a "kind" of president of a "kind" of company; he was also a prisoner for four years.), is because they will stay and fight rather than back down from what they see as important in the moment. They aren't always able to sense when to it's best to just keep quiet and go with the flow. They have to make a lot of noise which draws attention and then can land them in prison. It's part of what makes them outlaws/heroes. So when your hero gets to this part of the journey, it most likely won't be only the story events that mess things up for him. He's likely to do it to himself, as well.

The Approach to the Inmost Cave can take place over many scenes or chapters. This is the middle of your story, and you want to do everything you can to keep it from sagging. Here is where you may lose faith in your story because you don't exactly know what to do with it. But *The Approach* has any number of intense moments to keep your hero on his toes. Here are some of them:

1. *Obstacles on the Journey*

The outlaw/hero's motto, remember, is *Rules are made to be broken*. There will be obstacles throughout your story, many of them disguised as rules, and they should increase in severity with every scene. During the *Approach*, one purpose for the obstacles is to bond the hero and his allies as well as to cause the hero to find a more centered connection with himself so that he can move forward with a stronger sense of purpose, so that the upcoming *Ordeal* won't take him down.

2. *Strategies*

Some heroes seem fearless. They are motivated by something so deep, they don't even consider what might be inside the cave waiting for them. They're confident, often impulsive, and march into the cave without a look back. Others carefully plan their approach; they organize their thoughts and the members of their team, they gather their weapons and make sure they're in good shape, they consult their map often. According to Vogler, archetypal masks shift during the *Approach* as the hero assigns new functions to members of his team. The outlaw/hero's strategy, often unconsciously, is to disrupt, destroy or shock. This is their way of waking the rest of us up. They may have some archaic strategies, as resisting conventional means, they do what has worked for them in the past. But their archaic strategies are partly what wakes up their own selves. When a strategy doesn't work anymore, the outlaw has to try something new, something possibly a little more mature. For example, an outlaw-politician who is used to manipulating the other party, or even members of his own party, on a *Hero's Journey*, begins to realize that manipulation is no longer going to get him what he wants, and he has to be more creative. He may even end up examining what he wants in a new light.

3. *Consciousness of the Hero*

The journey is the hero's, but the shadow is never idle, even though he may be out of the hero's vision for a time. During the *Approach*, the shadow may threaten the hero in some way—what will happen if he continues to approach the *Cave*? The outlaw/hero's greatest fear is to be powerless or ineffectual. The shadow knows this, knows where the hero's weakness is and aims for just that area.

4. *Dramatic Complications, Higher Stakes, and the Impossible Test*

The *Approach* is the place to turn up the heat and make it really rough for your hero. Whatever the high stakes are, now is the time to raise them. Do you have a ticking clock in your story? At this stage, the complications he faces may discourage, dishearten, and depress him. But in the long run, these are the challenges that strengthen your hero's inner core. There is also one major test that he must face before he enters the *Cave*. What is it? Be creative.

5. *Illusions and Seductions*

Because the hero is often afraid at this stage, he can be more easily seduced and/or deceived by illusions—either by the work of others who oppose him or by his own mind. He doesn't want to believe that the journey is really a big deal, so he may play it down, deny it, pretend there is no journey, see a reality that isn't there, fall asleep at the helm.

6. *More Threshold Guardians*

Those who want to block your hero will come out in force at this stage. The hero is getting closer, so the threshold guardians become more desperate. Amidst setbacks, the hero grows in strength as the journey moves ahead, and part of his testing is to confront and overcome the opposition of the increasing strength and strategies of the threshold guardians. Sometimes it even takes getting into their minds or putting on their skin. A hero's threshold guardians understand that some rules have to be kept, regardless, and the value of the threshold guardians at this stage can be that the outlaw/hero begins to get that these characters are not necessarily against him, just against the dark side of him that won't bow to conventional wisdom under any circumstances. The outlaw/hero realizes that there is a time for everything; a time for anarchy and a time for peace. Eventually, if he's a true hero, he will come to know when it's time for what.

7. *Love and Intimacy*

One way the hero gathers his courage as he makes his *Approach* is with an intimate encounter with his wife or lover. This is the stage in movies where you'll often find the sex scene. These moments can strengthen him or have the opposite effect—tear him apart, especially if his sexual encounter is with a seductress who is up to no good. (Think Samson and Delilah.)

8. *Final moments*

Vogler calls the *Approach* "shaman's territory"—the edge of life and death which can create a kind of eerie, almost otherworldly mood in the story, no matter your story genre. One of your characters could be seriously hurt or even killed here. At this point, the doors behind him slam shut, your hero's fear of powerlessness accelerates, and he may be forced or force his way through that fear to the inmost cave. What will it take to get him to this place where he will let nothing stop him from moving ahead on the journey?

"Antagonists and heroes in conflict are like horses on a team pulling in different directions, while villains and heroes in conflict are like trains on a head-on collision course."

~ Chris Vogler

What are the obstacles the hero faces as he makes his Approach? What is his response?

What are the new functions the hero assigns to the members of his team?

Who is lost in the shuffle? Which of the characters in your story change their masks at this time?

Is your hero the type who confidently marches into the Cave? Or does he carefully plan, and what is his strategy?

How does the shadow threaten the hero, announcing the danger he's about to face?

What are your hero's dramatic complications? High stakes? Ticking clock? Impossible test?

Shadow's purpose:
Internal:

• to bring up the repressed aspects of the hero's psyche so that they can be integrated

• to create psychoses that threaten to destroy the hero's psyche

• to relentlessly confront the hero and provoke thought and emotion that leads to transformation

• to provide a mirror from within other characters so that the hero can see what he doesn't see

• to shelter positive qualities that the hero refuses to acknowledge or own

What are the seductions and illusions your hero could easily fall prey to?

Who are the threshold guardians as your hero approaches the Cave? How does your hero get into their minds and skin?

Does your hero have an intimate encounter at this stage? With whom and what happens?

How does your hero convince himself to move ahead into the Cave?

THE ROLE OF THE SHADOW

WHAT IS THE SHADOW BUT THE DARK ENERGY that shows up as the antagonist, the villain, the insanity in the hero's own psyche? Without a shadow, the hero has nothing to push against, no yardstick with which to measure himself, no conflict to provoke positive growth and transformation.

The shadow represents all of those dimmed places in the hero—unmet longings and desires, crazy fears and obsessions, unresolved shame and guilt, unacknowledged good and evil, repressed accomplishments and failures, avoidance of life and death. When he comes along, something in the hero rises up to fight to keep these elements of his personality hidden. As a physical presence, the shadow appears as the antagonist who will, at every turn, try to take our hero down. He's not a bad person; cutting the hero down is his role. He's just fulfilling his destiny. Betraying Jesus was not on Judas' daily to-do list; it was his destiny.

So, as you can see, while the shadow can be an evil villain (the worst part of our hero), he can also just be an antagonist who, because of his own agenda that opposes the hero's, brings the best out of the hero because of the confrontations that cause the hero to have to fight for what he wants and believes in. Externally, the shadow may be a character or force, while internally, it could be a deeply repressed energy force inside of the hero. The antagonist in your story does not at all need to be a completely evil force of energy; balance this character so that his humanity comes through. You want an antagonist the reader believes is true because he's real.

The most dangerous of shadows believe in their cause enough to die for it. The suicide bomber is a good example of this. On the other side is the shadow that brings out long-forgotten positive aspects of the hero's psyche. Sometimes, in order to do this, he provides a mirror from within other characters so that the hero can see what he doesn't see.

Because of the outlaw/hero's propensity to swim upstream and challenge conventional wisdom, he may see the shadow as a more positive character and feel guilty and full of shame whenever the shadow shows up. In this sense, the shadow doesn't appear as a villain, antagonist, or dark character at all, but as a creature of light. This would be true for the anti-hero or tragic hero story, as well. If a hero is more comfortable with his outlaw side than his hero side, the shadow can help balance his energy in a good way.

The hero confronts and defeats the external shadow (for a rewarding ending). In a story that's more internal, the hero integrates the shadow so that it becomes a part of his consciousness.

Shadow's purpose:
External:

• to show up in hero's dreams to provide the opportunity for the psyche to own and be reconciled to its unacceptable aspects

• to embarrass and humiliate the hero as it bursts out unannounced

• to come against the hero in a way that can not be ignored

• to thwart the hero's goal

• to push against the hero and create tension at every turn of the plot

• to overtake the hero so that the essence of his true self is paralyzed

• to shapeshift and throw the hero off balance

Who is the shadow in your story?

What is the role the shadow plays in his opposition of the hero and his goal?

Shadow energy:

• projects onto others

• works to keep unconscious aspects of psyche repressed

• represents the energy of rejected aspects, the dark side

• torments with doubt, guilt, and shame

• chases and stalks until dealt with—brought into light

• appears in dreams as monsters, demons, vampires, creepy characters

• becomes a mask for other archetypes

• exhausts as the struggle is often with an unseen force

• keeps the gold hidden

How does the shadow show vulnerability?

How does the shadow show up in a positive light for the outlaw/hero?

How does the shadow antagonize the hero and at the same time prod him to pursue his goal with even more effort?

What is the shadow's view of the story situation?

What is the shadow's personal agenda?

What are the weapons in the shadow's arsenal (tangible and non-tangible)?

How does the hero either defeat and/or integrate the shadow?

Famous Shadows:

The Grim Reaper

Darth Vader

Hannibal Lecter

Captain Hook

Tonya Harding

Cruella Deville

The Joker

BUSTING THE MYTH OF "WRITER'S BLOCK"

I PERSONALLY DON'T BELIEVE IN THE TRADITIONAL "WRITER'S BLOCK" as it's referred to in writing books and magazines, as writers have discussed it for years and years. It's been defined as this kind of ominous cloud that comes over us against our will and makes it impossible for us to write for days, weeks, sometimes months, and even years. I've heard writers blame and project all of their writing inadequacies and self-doubts onto this nebulous writer's disease called "writer's block." I'm not sure when I started to suspect that WB wasn't at all the cause for that stuck feeling we suffer from time to time, that it was an easy scapegoat we could use as an excuse as long as we liked, as long as we couldn't or didn't want to inquire any further or deeper to try to find out what the real issues were that kept us from putting pen to paper and later, sitting down at the computer.

But writer's block is a myth. Whenever we can't write, it's about one thing and one thing only—it's the shadow in our unconscious hiding a very specific wound needing inquiry and then healing and integration. It's true that we're blocked, but it, in and of itself, is not the problem, just the symptom. And as long as we keep labeling that stuck feeling as writer's block, we won't actively do anything about it. We become passive, just waiting for it to go away on its own. One day we may wake up and feel like writing again. Or not. But without inquiring into what's causing us to feel stuck, we're missing out on an opportunity to deepen our writing, to learn to write more authentically.

Think about the last time you felt stuck in your writing. Feeling stuck is the condition. Underneath the condition is a reason. It's up to you as a writer to investigate the reason. It may have something to do with what you're writing, it may not. For some reason, you've lost your voice.

I have a friend, Greg, whose address happens to be a Washington State Prison. He writes novels, or I should say "wrote" novels until one day a couple of Correction Officers did one of those cell strips where they nabbed everything he owned and only gave some of it back. One of the things he didn't get back was 400 pages of his work-in-progress. Other than letters, he didn't write anything for 15 years. He calls it writer's block. I call it fear. Can we blame him? If he were to begin writing again, he would have to live totally in the moment with his writing. Write, release. Write, release. Write, release. He could never become attached to his writing again, because he knows that at any moment, it could be taken from him. He's recently started writing his memoir; after writing a few pages, he immediately sends them to loved ones on the outside to keep for him.

I would imagine that it's difficult for you, as an outlaw, to acknowledge fear of any kind, not just because of where you're living at the moment, but because you might be looking at fear as a weakness, and you certainly don't want to feel weak. But fear is simply an emotion, a natural response to feeling threatened in some way. And even if there aren't guards outside the door ready to strip your cell and steal your writing, you'll still have moments of feeling fear because fear is inside of us. We are our own worst enemy at times which means we can actually create that threatening feeling inside of ourselves. It's part of being human for writers, this thing we call writer's block. Sky divers have fear. Public speakers have fear. Bank robbers have fear. As a writer, can you identify what your fear is all about that's causing you to feel unable to write?

If you've ever experienced writer's block, if you're experiencing it now, I wish I had the answer for you. But there's only one person who has the answer, and that person needs to resist the label, writer's block, and instead, start asking what that stuck feeling is all about and what it would take to begin to freely write again.

ASSIGNMENT:

WRITE A DRAMATIC SCENE OR A NARRATIVE SUMMARY of your hero's *Approach to the Inmost Cave*. What is he most afraid of as he makes his approach? Does he disguise himself before he goes inside? If so, what is the mask that he puts on? Who does he meet at the cave's entrance? More threshold guardians? Shapeshifters? The shadow? Does he run headlong into the cave, or does he carefully plan his strategy? What does this stage call up from him internally?

1) Please choose one of the following options:

• Write a short *Approach to the Inmost Cave* scene of 1000 or fewer words

• Write one scene and a summary of the other scenes in *The Approach to the Inmost Cave*

• Write a summary of all of the scenes in the *Approach to the Inmost Cave* stage of the journey

2) Create a profile for your shadow in 300 or fewer words. Emphasize, not the details of his appearance, but the answers to the above questions in our section on the shadow. Focus specifically on his role in *The Hero's Journey*. How does he oppose the hero in his goals while furthering his own? What makes his personal goal so crucially important to him? What is his greatest weakness, that one thing that can bring him to his knees? Consider how a shadow might influence an outlaw/hero.

3) Consider a subject that is terrifying for you to write about. The more you can write about those topics that terrify you, the less you'll experience blocks as a writer. Write 500 words on the topic of your choice, refusing

to back down from the scariest parts of your topic. If you're blocked in a fictional story you're writing, pick a scene and use those 500 words to write into your hero's greatest fear.

LESSON EIGHT

THE ORDEAL, THE ROLE OF THE SHAPESHIFTER, AND IDENTIFYING YOUR THEME

IT OFTEN SEEMS THAT LIFE IS ONE ORDEAL after another, or maybe I'm just an Eyore rather than a Pooh, but it seems true, and so it's difficult, if you're looking at your entire life as a *Hero's Journey*, to choose just one ordeal to highlight in your story. But if you're writing a memoir or a novel, or even a short story or a short personal experience story, you want to cover just one area of your character's or your own life, which means picking just one *Ordeal* to develop as a scene and use to internally transform your hero.

If, say, I were writing a story about my relationship with my ex-husband, I'm not sure, er, if the *Ordeal* would be the marriage or the divorce. If you were writing about your life as an outlaw, your *Ordeal* might be your arrest. The end of your game. It all depends on the scope of your story. If you wanted to write about the *Hero's Journey* that is prison, the *Ordeal* would be that moment inside where you face the greatest test of your will, where you can choose one of two paths—that of outlaw/hero or that of tragic hero. You don't have to choose between outlaw and hero as the goal is to integrate the outlaw archetype and the hero archetype. This means developing that moment in your story where you know that even though you remain an outlaw, you will do it within the perimeters the law sets for you. A good example of this is the late Dr. Jack Kevorkian, the doctor who helped many people die before being arrested and prosecuted. After that, he had a habit of saying in interviews, when asked if he would help people die again, "Only if I have power within the law to assist them in ending their lives." Internally, after he was released from prison, he was still an outlaw.

THE ORDEAL

THIS STAGE IS ONE OF THE MOST TENSE of all of the stages and one of the biggest crises the hero will face in the story. It can come halfway through, or it can be a delayed crisis and come about three-fourths of the way through. It's the moment when the hero's literal life hangs in the balance. He must face some kind of death at this point—emotional, spiritual, mental, or psychological. The purpose of this moment is so that he can resurrect, taking his lessons from the special world back to the *Ordinary World.*

The hero's death shouldn't be a literal one. (A movie like *Psycho* comes along once in a lifetime and only by a master like Alfred Hitchcock.) Too many new writers, for some reason, want to kill off their heroes. Maybe they think it's the ultimate in drama and will assure the success of their stories. This isn't the case. All this does is reveal that these writers are novices. No, the hero's encounter with death can be the facing of his greatest fear, the failure to succeed at his most important goal, the final loss of a relationship, the death of a former and unhealthy part of the hero's personality. It could also be the physical death of a loved one.

At this stage, the hero must call up all of his resources to face down his external and internal demons. Here is where he remembers the lessons learned from his mentor and is able to use them.

The major goal of the outlaw/hero archetype is to destroy what's not working for either himself or society, and his greatest fear is to be inconsequential or trivialized. Because of this, the *Ordeal* is a pivotal moment for an outlaw and holds, perhaps, at least the beginning of his biggest lesson in the story. Here is where he makes his greatest effort to achieve his goal and where he must face down his major fear. At this stage of your story, you want to work on your hero's character arc while also coming up with the biggest external obstacle, the most monstrous dragon yet for him to slay. Consider how the other characters in the story might find our hero of no significant value, how they might trivialize his ideas, disrespect him in some way, while simultaneously getting him to the point where he feels desperate enough to try to destroy what's not working in his own life or in society. Whether or not he's seeing everything clearly is really beside the point—he sees what he sees. There will be sacrifices made, possibly a fatality, some casualties of battle—both internally and externally. If you're writing a personal story, think of the time when you were backed against the wall, more desperate than you'd ever been to prove yourself—to yourself, to everyone around you. The hero often feels like a lone ranger at this point.

In the *Ordeal*, the hero often faces off in some kind of emotional, psychological or physical battle with the antagonist. Here, the shadow character embodies the unconscious fears and weaknesses of the hero in human form, and so if the hero kills the shadow, he is killing that part of himself and so is taking responsibility for his own ultimate transformation.

What is your Hero's Journey's central crisis?

What does the outlaw/hero feel he needs to destroy? How does he feel inconsequential and/or trivialized?

What happens between the shadow and the hero during the Ordeal? What does the shadow bring up for the hero that must die?

How is it that your hero appears to die and what brings him back from the edge?

How does the Ordeal change your hero forever?

THE ROLE OF THE SHAPESHIFTER

Shapeshifter's purpose:

Internal:

• to challenge and call into question the hero's perceptions of the other characters

• to reflect the hero's unspoken desire for transformation

• to promote new understanding of the restrained energies within the hero

• to challenge the reader and hero to question beliefs and assumptions

• to project with a personal agenda

• to create mental and emotional chaos in the hero's psyche

• to cause the hero to distrust his own gut about what he sees, hears, senses

JOHN PERKINS, THE AUTHOR OF *SHAPESHIFTING: Shamanic Techniques for Global and Personal Transformation* writes that we need intent, energy, and action, that it's only when these three human forces are in place that we can have true shapeshifting.

Why would you *want* "true shapeshifting"? To throw the hero into doubt and the story into suspense. In the hero's point of view, this is an ever-changing character, not to be trusted because you never know who he or she is going to be or where he or she is going to turn up next. This is a character who morphs in physical, emotional and/or mental energy. The hero's perception of the shapeshifter may or may not be true—it really doesn't matter because he believes his own perceptions, whatever they are.

According to Vogler, Shapeshifters often have to do with the hero's perceptions of the opposite sex—who that person is, really, and whether he or she is for or against the hero. Many of romance's deepest conflicts between couples could possibly be navigated more easily if each person understood the dynamics of the shapeshifter in the relationship and how it plays out in the couple's interaction.

Shapeshifters have many roles:

• They challenge and call into question the hero's perceptions of the other characters

• They reflect the hero's unspoken desire for transformation while remaining fickle about and uncommitted to the hero's cause and goal

• They promote new understanding of the restrained energies within the hero

- They challenge the reader and hero to question beliefs and assumptions, at times dazzling the hero, at other times, confusing or seducing him

- They project with a personal agenda

- They create mental and emotional chaos in the hero's psyche

- They cause the hero to distrust his own gut about what he sees, hears, senses

- They remind the hero that nothing is as it appears to be, while simultaneously seeing the potential in everything

The shapeshifter keeps the hero guessing, keeps him wondering about what's true in the story situation. Any character can wear the mask of the shapeshifter at any time, in order to get past an obstacle or a threshold guardian. The hero himself becomes a shapeshifter at times in order to move ahead on the journey.

The sports marketing agency, *Active Imagination*, defines the outlaw in some depth on their website: *In the beginning, the outlaw dissociates him or herself from society in a way that shocks and confronts conventional values. At the deepest level of the archetype, the outlaw uses his or her power to disrupt the system to become a true revolutionary, overturning obsolete or ineffective establishments in order to create a new order.*

This is pertinent to developing the outlaw/hero protagonist as a shapeshifter because in order to "disrupt the system" in a way that's effective, our hero may have to shift his shape and morph into another form in order to accomplish his goal. So, for example, our outlaw/hero may don a business suit and become an employee of a company that he sees as harming society, and then once he gets inside, begins to question and challenge all business strategies so that changes can be made. Or, say, you want to intensify the journey for the hero who's refusing the *Call*, you

Shapeshifter's purpose:

External:

• to shift from side to side during the story, throw the hero off balance

• to delay the hero on his journey

• to dazzle and confuse the hero

• to bring uncertainty and tension into the story events

• to change form to get past an obstacle in the story

• to cause the hero to distrust his loyalty and sincerity

• to reveal a lack of commitment to and fickleness about the hero's causes and goal in story may create a character who wears a wire to catch the hero in whatever shady practices he's up to before he accepts his role as hero. The shapeshifter's role is always to throw the hero off balance.

Shapeshifter energy:

• is the anima/animus balance of the psyche

• shifts view of reality

• reminds that nothing is as it appears to be

• shifts in mood, appearance, behavior

• reveals itself as deviousness or lying

• possesses the ability to navigate

• sees potential in everything

• reveals a lack of conviction

Who is the shapeshifter in your story?

What is his or her role in the hero's situation and his goal?

How does your shapeshifter provoke the hero and keep him off balance?

What is your shapeshifter's view of the story situation?

What is your shapeshifter's personal agenda?

What are the masks your shapeshifter wears and how does he use them to confuse the hero?

Famous Shapeshifters:

Wicked Queen in Snow White

The Wizard of Oz

Han Solo

David Bowie

Delilah

Any politician

Is your shapeshifter friend or foe? Or both?

IDENTIFYING YOUR THEME

AT SOME POINT, YOU NEED TO KNOW what your *Hero's Journey* story is really all about. The hero's major internal conflict and insight that leads to resolution is what's called your *theme*. It's the story's central truth that sometimes may come to you even before you begin to write your story, but most often emerges *as* you write. Your story's central truth is often illusive, trying to hide from you. It's *supposed* to do that. Your job is to write into your theme, to coax it out of your story. If you complete the first draft, read it back over, and the theme still seems to be missing, then your job isn't yet finished.

This is the work. As a writing coach, this is where I see writers resist, more than at any other part of the writing process. There are several reasons for this:

1. Digging out one's theme *is* work, and the writer is afraid that, after all is said and done, there's really nothing of substance there

2. The writer may unconsciously know his theme but not want to bring it out in the open because then he'll be responsible for living it out

3. The theme may be one that the writer is ashamed or embarrassed to acknowledge or confront

4. The theme is buried in the shadow and may be one that is painful to acknowledge

If you find yourself resisting theme, be gentle with yourself. Most of us resist, at least at first. It's often part of the writing process. But it's worth the work to inquire into your theme, because this is where writer and reader truly connect. We may experience similar situations, approach our lives in similar ways, have like challenges, but finding meaning in those situations and challenges is what connects all of us. As you write your ending, when you're ready to sign off, your theme will begin to peek out. Pay attention so that you don't miss it.

Begin to ponder what you might want your story to say. Stephen King, in his memoir, On Writing, says, "…it seems to me that every book—at least every one worth reading—is about *something*. Your job during or just after the first draft is to decide what something or somethings yours is about."

Personally, I think hard about theme before I ever start to write a story. It saves a lot of rewriting later and is much easier for me to keep my story on track when I know what I'm writing about. To create your theme is to consider your story's truth, its major conflict and resolution—both external and internal. The main character—you, if it's a personal story, your protagonist, if it's fiction—is the one who plays out the theme and delivers the story's "message" to the reader. I remember watching the movie, *The Interpreter*, where one of the main characters says to the other one, *"Vengeance is a lazy form of grief."* I knew when she said it, that it was the theme, and as the story played out, it became more clear that the real story underneath all of the car chases and shoot-'em-up scenes was about how to grieve without taking revenge on those who hurt us. Another theme I really like comes from The Pirates of the Caribbean. Governor Swann stands tall and says boldly: *"Perhaps on the rare occasion that the right course demands an act of piracy, piracy itself can be the right course."* This is a typical theme for an outlaw/hero story.

As an outlaw, the theme in your story may be one that's difficult for you to articulate because you've been ostracized from society, set apart, now in exile, at least in part because at some level, you were willing to go outside of the law to get what you wanted, to stand up for what you thought was right, to succeed at something illegal. Even if you simply lost control of yourself in a moment and committed a horrible atrocity against another person, at some level, some part of you felt you had a right to do that, or you wouldn't have done it. Our themes are those values and beliefs and worldviews that give our lives meaning and purpose. The fact that you're in prison could mean that your world view may need to be tweaked a bit, but don't throw it completely out. Find out what drives you as the hero of your story, your protagonist as the hero of his story, and then it's your job to find a way to subtlely and expertly craft it, integrating it into all of your scenes so that it doesn't ever really show.

ASSIGNMENT:

Write a dramatic scene or a narrative summary of your hero's *Ordeal*. If he's an outlaw, what is it that he feels compelled to destroy in the story, something that will ultimately improve his life and the whole of society, though he may not even be aware of his impact? What happens during this stage in his encounter with the shadow—internally and externally? How does he appear to die, and how is he changed forever as a result of enduring *The Ordeal*?

1) Please choose one of the following options:

* Write a short *Ordeal* scene of 1000 or fewer words

* Write one scene and a summary of the other scenes in *The Ordeal* stage

* Write a summary of all of the scenes in *The Ordeal* stage of the journey

2) Create a profile for your shapeshifter in 300 or fewer words. Emphasize, not the details of his appearance, but the answers to the above questions in our section on the shapeshifter. Focus specifically on his role in the *Hero's Journey*. How does he shape shift so as to throw the hero off his game? What is the disguise or mask he wears so that the hero is confused and his moral code tested? What is his personal agenda for doing what he does?

3) Ponder what you think your story might be about. You may or may not know at this point, so just do the best you can. You can get to your theme by asking yourself some questions. What inspired you to write this

particular story? What is the hero's major conflict leading to the insight—
the hero's truth? Write a short scene—500 or fewer words—where the
hero or another character states, thinks or acts out the story's theme/truth.

LESSON NINE

THE REWARD, THE ROLE OF THE TRICKSTER, & TENSION, SUSPENSE, AND PACING

THE HERO'S REWARD TOWARDS THE END OF THE JOURNEY comes in all shapes and sizes. It can be external (getting the girl) or internal (a deep acceptance of something he can't change). You want to be creative in how you write this part of your story, as you don't want the reward to be a predictable one.

I remember seeing a movie, the ending of which sticks with me to this day. In the last scene, it was the look on the anti-hero's face—a lawyer who had fiercely defended his client, going back and forth and around with him throughout the movie, but in the end, absolutely sure of his innocence. It was clear the client was a master manipulator and shapeshifter, but we weren't worried about it because the attorney was also a master manipulator and shapeshifter and very smart. Smarter than his client, for sure. We thought.

It's the client's parting shot, spoken in his quiet way, as the attorney leaves the jail after visiting him for the last time before the trial. He's just been had. Big time. In a way that everyone will know--and this attorney's image is ultra-important to him.

The reward? Wisdom. The kind of wisdom one can only learn by engaging with someone a little smarter than oneself. A little wiser in the ways of the world, even if that wisdom is revealed in a horrible crime. Our anti-hero will never be the same. He may even be able to integrate his own outlaw archetype in this moment if he's truly on a *Hero's Journey*. We don't know because the movie doesn't take us beyond this moment.

One reason we sometimes come away from movies shaking our heads is because we don't like the reward the hero receives. He didn't earn it, and it bugs us. *The Reward* should always be one that the hero earns by making sacrifices and taking risks. He deserves it because he's worked hard.

THE REWARD (SEIZING THE SWORD)

THIS STAGE IS ABOUT SUFFERING the consequences and/or reaping the rewards of surviving the *Ordeal*—metaphorical or literal death. One of my favorite *Hero's Journey* stories of all time is Philippe Petit's tightrope walk between the twin towers in New York in 1974. *Man on Wire* beautifully documents Petit's journey from beginning to end as he prepared to take the longest and scariest and most magnificent walk of his life. I was mesmerized as I watched the entire documentary, but I can't watch *The Reward* part without a gentle and poignant kind of crying—I'm just so moved at all that led up to this one moment on the wire and then right afterwards,

After years of preparation, Petit's whole life, actually, our outlaw/hero steps out on the cable he and his "assistants" have strung from one tower to the next. And what a step it is. He has worked so hard to get to this one moment, and I'm biting my nails, sure he's about to plunge to a violent death. Even after watching the documentary several times, I don't see how it could have happened any other way. Every time, I wonder if my eyes are deceiving me as he does the impossible. Is it magic? He doesn't only step out on the wire, he sits down, he lies down, he does a little dance. He was only going to cross one time, but when he sees the police, he's suddenly inspired to put on a show, and he crosses seven more times! But the first time across is the most moving. He defies gravity and all convention and our very eyes. Those on the ground look up and are stunned to see a human figure crossing a cable between the twin towers. This one act captures everyone's attention, for in that one moment we all know and share the knowledge that anything is possible, if we just believe we can do it. A man can walk on wire. We can do anything. We can be anything.

The walk is coming to an end. Petit has taunted the police, in public nonetheless, and now they're seriously after him. Threshold guardians to be sure, but it's too late. They're powerless to stop him. He has slain his dragons, faced his greatest fear in the inmost cave, and accomplished his journey. *The Road Back* (next lesson) is loud and chaotic as he steps off the wire, and the police and the crowd descend on him, not to congratulate him and drape him in the cloak of a hero, but to gawk at him as a freak who just broke some obscure law and committed "The Artistic Crime of the Century" (Time Magazine).

There is a time in every *Hero's Journey* when the hero is on his own, and for Philippe Petit, this seems to be that time. What is *The Reward* for your hero as he nears the end of his journey? It must be something that an outlaw would see as a reward. He wouldn't necessarily find a new car or winning the lottery much of a reward. But to earn the respect of his homies. Or his family. To discover that he's made a difference in some kid's life. To have saved a damsel in distress so that she can have a happy life, even though he had to break the law to do it. You and I both know that there are many right there in prison with you who would commit their particular crime all over again to reap *The Reward* they've received. Maybe you're one of those.

Definitely the outlaw, in Philippe Petit's, case, it was literal death—107 floors between Petit and the ground as he crossed between the towers. This is where the hero is acknowledged and recognized, often celebrating with friends and family. The *Man on Wire's* first celebration ceremony was with the police—after stepping back onto the building, he was immediately arrested. Then a huge number of reporters appeared. Celebrating in jail. Ugh.

Still, our wirewalker-hero experiences the sweet smell of victory in his jail cell, and nothing can take it away from him, even this endurance test. Fortunately, his partner-in-crime, Jean-Francois, is with him, and they participate in the rituals of storytelling, boasting, nostalgia, and joke telling after the *Ordeal*.

In this stage, the hero is taking possession of whatever it was that his journey has been about thus far. He metaphorically seizes the sword— he has battled his enemies and survived, he finds his voice, he recovers his life. *The Reward* can be something physical, or it can be a spiritual or psychological epiphany. Some heroes purchase *The Reward* by sacrificing something that means a lot to them, and some outlaw/heroes steal it. Philippe Petit stole it. Either way, the victory couldn't be sweeter because of the effort put in.

During *The Reward* stage, the other characters often see the hero in a new, more positive light and respond to him differently than they did before. They may have a newfound respect for him. Threshold guardians begin to align themselves with him.

After facing death, our hero is a different person. This could include some distorted perceptions and an inflated sense of self leading to some mistakes along the way as he grapples with the new person that he's become on the journey. It takes time to integrate all of the lessons he's learned up until this point, and his shadow may trip him up a bit right after the exhilaration of the journey. At the same time, he's wiser, and during the process of integration, his perceptions, powers of observation, and moments of clarity are sharper than ever before.

Finally, a few hours after being arrested, the charges against Philippe Petit are dropped, and he is free to go. According to Christopher Vogler, part of this stage can include a love scene. Again, *Man On Wire* provides us with a classic example. After being released from jail, Instead of running back to his longtime lover, Annie, he responds to the attention of a young girl in the crowd who has watched his wire walking act. They rent a hotel room where they make love. This moment in Petit's journey signifies that he's a changed man. While we don't know all that went into Petit's spontaneous moment of debauchery as he took possession of this part of his reward, he describes it as *revenge and abandon, an immense joy, the warmest entanglement, an ephemeral delirium of the senses.* Then he says, *…after all the questions, exhausted, elated, I need, I deserve, I want the first step in my new life to be splashed with decadence, an explosion of passions.*

I feel compelled to acknowledge that if you're a lifer and writing a personal story, *The Reward* part of your story might be a little challenging for you. If you're not getting out of prison, if you'll never be externally free, where's *The Reward?* I don't mean to minimize or trivialize this part of the journey for you, but if your goal is ultimately your freedom from prison, the reward would be actually to surrender to reality inside of your innermost being where there's a peace you'll never know as long as you're still striving and flailing. I'm speaking to myself as well even though I'm out here in the supposedly "free world." To be honest, while I've met many lifers, I've never yet met one that seemed to be flailing. The ones I've met may be waiting for a miracle—their freedom—but they know in their heart of hearts that their true freedom doesn't depend on their release from prison. The true reward always includes a release, not from prison, but from wanting. Craving. Okay, I guess, in truth, that *is* a release from prison.

What is your hero's reward for having survived the Ordeal? What is he now in possession of? Is The Reward something that an outlaw/hero would highly value, and how is that true?

How does the hero defuse the tension in the story during The Reward stage?

Is there a love scene for your hero at this stage? With whom? What happens?

What is the real meaning of The Reward now in our hero's possession? How is he a changed person? What are the epiphanies that have opened up his world for him?

Do any of your story's threshold guardians see your hero differently at this stage? How do their roles in his journey change?

Does your hero experience an inflated sense of self or anything else that could create a few problems for him before he balances out and is able to integrate everything he experienced on the journey?

Trickster energy:

- causes impish accidents
- makes slips of the tongue
- symbolizes monkey mind
- creates chaos when things seem too orderly
- sees flaws in status quo, hypocrisy in other characters, is willing to criticize or mock even his friends
- crosses boundaries
- drops in, provokes change, moves on

Famous Tricksters:

Bugs Bunny

Woody Woodpecker

Bill Maher

Bart Simpson

David Letterman

Madonna

Br'er Rabbit

How will you show that your hero's perceptions, powers of observation, and moments of clarity are sharper than ever before?

THE ROLE OF THE TRICKSTER

Trickster's purpose:

External:

• to provide comic relief, create a break from tension

• to speed up the story

• to twist the story

• to challenge reader to question conventional wisdom

• to keep the hero honest, even while possibly being dishonest himself

• to keep the hero's head from getting too big

• to provide a cynical view of story situation

IN MYTHOLOGY, AND IN THE STUDY OF FOLKLORE AND RELIGION, a trickster is a god, goddess, spirit, man, woman, or anthropomorphic animal who plays tricks or otherwise disobeys normal rules and conventional behavior. (Wikipedia) In storytelling, he's the character who survives in a dangerous world through use of trickery. In *The Hero's Journey*, through cleverness and wit, he's able to help the hero shift his perception of the situation. He keeps the protagonist honest even while possibly being dishonest himself.

The trickster is a jokester. Nothing is too serious with him. He can cut a hero's ego down to size in a moment. He points out folly and hypocrisy and makes both hero and reader laugh at themselves. Because he's so good at perceiving the absurdity of convention and rigid rule keeping, he's the natural enemy of the status quo. He's not afraid to confront or criticize those who take themselves too seriously, even when they're his close friends. He tends to have a cynical view of the story situation, and he might be aligned with either the hero or the shadow, or he might be all on his own with his own skewed agenda.

Trickster energy can both twist and speed up a story. It's mischievous and can cause impish accidents and create chaos when things seem too orderly. Boundaries are often crossed when the trickster drops in, provokes change and moves on.

While tricksters are often irresponsible, sexually over-active, and amoral in how they behave, on a higher level, they also represent a certain flexibility of mind and spirit, a willingness to defy authority and invent clever solutions that keeps cultures (and stories) from becoming too stagnant.

If your hero has a strong outlaw archetype, how are you going to make the trickster different enough to present other options when the hero is confused and needing to make a decision? How are you going to show the trickster bouncing off the walls when your outlaw/hero is already doing that? This is the challenge. If your outlaw/hero is out of control, you may have to tone your trickster down so that he presents the voice of reason, still in a comic or edgy way.

Who is your trickster? How does he bring laughter, a smile, comic relief to the hero on his journey?

What is the relationship between your hero and the trickster?

Is your trickster an outlaw, and how does he challenge conventional wisdom in your story?

Trickster's purpose:

Internal:

• to cut the hero's ego down to size

• to help the reader realize common bonds

• to point out folly and hypocrisy

• to bring about healthy change and transformation

• to bring needed perspective so that no one in the story takes himself too seriously

• to oppose, mock, challenge, question, and/or work against the status quo

• to represent a certain flexibility of mind and spirit, a willingness to defy authority and invent clever solutions that keeps cultures (and stories) from becoming too stagnant.

TIGHTENING THE TENSION

I ONCE TAUGHT A CLASS AT A WRITERS CONFERENCE where I passed out a box of rubber bands and asked everyone to take one. I then asked the audience to stretch their rubber bands. That's tension," I said. Then I told them to aim their rubber bands at the person next to them. "That's how you tighten the tension," I told them.

To tighten the tension is to create a bit—or a lot--of anxiety in your story. It's to raise the stakes for the hero. It's to create doubt about a positive outcome to the conflict. It's to throw all of the characters out of their comfort zones and make the reader wonder whether the hero will reach his goal. It's to horrify, anger and/or grieve the reader. It's to make everyone—characters and reader—a little uneasy.

The tension should be tightened notch by notch through the story—a little here, a lot there. A scene without tension is a scene that doesn't work and where the reader stops reading. You can count on it. The large number of novels and memoirs that I start reading and don't finish each year are ones where the author fails to sustain the tension.

When plotting, you only want to stop and develop those scenes where the characters have found a place of tension, where they disagree about something. Even a scene where two characters are robbing a bank, though dramatic, will only include tension if those characters disagree about exactly how the bank should be robbed, whether it should be approached from the front or the rear, whether, they should pretend to have a gun or whether they should have a real one, whether they should run away from the scene on foot, or whether they should use a getaway car. If there are customers in the bank, we know there will be a bit of conflict there already between the bank customers and the gunmen—the customers won't appreciate being told by a masked gunman to hit the floor and lay still when they simply walked into the bank to cash a check or make a deposit.

Tension in the literary, mainstream or personal life story, once again, largely comes from within the characters; how they perceive the story events differently from each other, how they react or respond to one another, if they choose to internalize their feelings or express them to one another.

It's a challenge sometimes to try to figure out exactly how to get tension into a story. But the one thing there's no doubt about—it has to be there, in every scene, in every moment of every scene. The character must want something he can't get, stand to lose something important, be deathly afraid of something. This is tension.

BUILDING THE SUSPENSE

MOST GENRE WRITERS KNOW THE VALUE OF SUSPENSE. When working with these writers, I don't usually have to try to convince them that they need suspense in their stories. But too many memoir, literary and mainstream writers seem to think that their story's voice or entertaining characters can carry the story, that that's enough to keep the reader turning the pages. I often wonder if they even think at all about ways to create suspense in their stories.

Every story needs suspense. Every scene in your story should be foreshadowing events and situations to come in the story that are scary, tense, and challenging for the hero. Of course, in a memoir or personal life story, that hero is you. You know what's going to happen in your story, so the suspense isn't there for you as you write. But your reader hasn't lived your life. In each scene, be sure to foreshadow the events to come so that the reader is engaged in your present conflicts and the outcome of those conflicts.

You create suspense in three ways:

1) Crafting your scenes and sequels (Lesson Four) so that they build on one another

2) Making sure your viewpoint character's goal is clear in each scene so that there is a specific outcome to be expected

3) Keeping the shadow busy

The stories of our lives are one suspenseful event after another. We think we have one problem solved when another comes at us in full force. Someone seems to finally be in recovery from drug addiction, but then someone else gets in a car accident. As a prison inmate, you may learn that you're finally getting your case appealed, only to find out that your lawyer is bailing on you or there's some other snag with the DOC. It's endless. Okay, it's been endless for me, at least. When considering the themes for our stories, we put all of these events together so that each conflict builds on the one before and foreshadows the one to come. You sustain suspense in any story when there is genuine doubt as to the outcome of each conflict. Will it end with everyone living happily ever after? Or not?

Give your hero (yourself, if it's a personal story) a very specific, very *measurable* goal in the very beginning of each scene. Unless a character's goal is clear, there's no way to know whether he has achieved what's so important to him. Make sure that the reader understands what it would look like if the goal is achieved and if it isn't. Be clear about what's at stake if it's not achieved, what the character stands to lose. Take the stakes just as high as you can and still keep the story believable. And show us how the character cares desperately about achieving his goal. In the genre story, such as the suspense thriller, the goal is to stay a step ahead of the bad guys(s). In the literary, memoir, and mainstream, the goal is internal as well as external and more complicated than staying ahead of the bad guys of whom are usually those close by. Just remember the word, *measurable*.

Your shadow character should have a long to-do list. That's his role. That's his job. As long as your shadow is stirring up trouble, there will be no lack of suspense in your story. Because whatever he does, it's always against the hero and whatever he wants in the story. As long as your hero's and shadow's agendas keep colliding, suspense is not something you'll ever have to worry about.

I do have one caveat: Don't create suspense just for the sake of creating suspense. Whatever kind of suspense you create does need to connect to what you're building in the plot and fit within the genre in which you're writing.

PACING YOUR STORY

A STORY DOES NOT PACE ITSELF. Characters don't pace the story. The story situation doesn't set the pace. So then what causes the story to ebb and flow? You do. If a story either drags or moves too quickly, the author is the only one at fault. You position your scenes in such a way so as to create a rhythm that works for the particular story you're writing. You speed a scene up or slow it down, to be determined by the overall rhythm you're trying to achieve. And the overall rhythm is most often determined by the genre. Action/adventure, suspense thrillers, horror stories, mysteries, and sci-fi/fantasies need to move along at a nice clip. The character-driven stories—personal life stories, literary and mainstream stories—can, but don't have to, move at a more leisurely pace.

The truth is, most stories move, not too quickly, but too slowly. In my work as a writing coach, maybe one in 200 stories that I read move too quickly. In the stories that move too quickly, the writer fails to develop scenes and characters, simply speeding from one scene to the next. The scenes are sometimes only two or three paragraphs long. Just as we're starting to get into what's going on with the characters, the scene is over and we're into the next scene.

As I mentioned, stories that move too slowly are much more common, and I see five major reasons for this.

1. The writer wants to use the story to philosophize or communicate a personal truth, so uses too much narrative to show the characters' emotion or lofty thoughts about life.

2. The writer is uncomfortable with conflict in real life, so fails to develop it in the story to any degree that includes suspense or action.

3. The writer starts the story with an unrealistic sense of just how many scenes it takes to maintain the momentum and suspense, ending up having to pad the story with rambling narrative.

4. The writer focuses on the characters' internal life rather than giving the reader the action needed to sustain ongoing interest and suspense.

5. The writer wants to make sure the reader has all of the necessary background about all of the characters before the action can continue.

To keep your story moving at a nice clip, you want to create scenes of action for your characters. Use lots of dialogue to keep things lively and weave narrative into the action only when it becomes necessary and is relevant to the present moment's conflict.

SURPRISING YOUR READER

I'VE WORKED WITH MANY WRITERS who don't think about their readers at all. I have to believe that's why some stories are so predictable. We know what's going to happen moment by moment. We've read it many times before. We know the good guys are going to win, the hero's going to get the girl, the suspect will get caught. This kind of story is no fun for the reader and you can bet that he will probably put it down before he's finished it.

There should be a surprise around every corner in your story. But before there can be a surprise, we should probably identify what a surprise is. Sexual abuse and homosexuality used to shock us. Guess what? Not anymore. These are no longer surprises. They can certainly still be elements in a story, but as a surprise for the reader—I don't think so. It would come as more of a surprise if a character announced she wanted to become a nun or a Buddhist. Can you imagine the surprise the reader would feel if a character announced she came from a good home and was never sexually abused? What a shock.

Let's be creative in thinking of ways to surprise the reader. Surprises don't have to necessarily be big things, either. A character's unusual quirk can create surprise after surprise in a story. Did you see the movie, *As Good as it Gets*? That character kept surprising us with his quirky compulsions and obsessions. In one of my favorite novels of all time, *The Confederacy of Dunces*, the anti-hero, Ignatius J. Reilly, keeps us in suspense as we wonder what ridiculous thing he is going to do next. What will he say to humiliate himself and everyone else? What crazy outfit will he wear? Where will he go and who will he meet? The author keeps surprising us. The same is true in the literary classic, *Catcher in the Rye*. It's so amazing to me how Holden Caulfield's thoughts are what keep us turning the pages. There is a new surprise on each page—all inside of his head.

The surprising elements in the life of an outlaw, whether fiction or nonfiction, might be revealed through his goodness, the ways he contributes something positive to society as well as the unconventional and illegal, which is what we've come to expect from this archetype. Think out of the box.

It's not that difficult to keep surprising the reader. You simply have to dig a little deeper, think a little harder about what makes your characters and their story situation just a little different. I watched a true crime story on television recently where the psychotic murderer killed her victims in an original way—putting antifreeze into their lime Jell-O. I believe that the instant success of a television show like *Desperate Housewives* (I'm guessing this wasn't one of your favorites, but if I'm thinking out of the box, maybe it might have been) can be directly attributed to its surprising twists and turns in every episode. You could never predict where it was going to go next. That's what you're after in surprising the reader—unpredictability, keeping both characters and readers off center just a bit.

Tightening the tension, creating suspense, pacing your story so that it moves, surprising the reader—you've got a big job as a storyteller.

ASSIGNMENT:

WRITE A DRAMATIC SCENE OR A NARRATIVE SUMMARY of your hero's *Reward*. Is it physical, financial, sexual? Emotional, intellectual, relational? There can be more than one reward. How is the tension defused at this stage? Does your hero have an inflated sense of self that will need balancing out before the end of the story? Do the other characters see him differently, and how? Be sure to show that your hero's perceptions, powers of observation, and moments of clarity are in some tangible way sharper than they were before.

1) Please choose one of the following options:

- Write a short *Reward* scene of 1000 or fewer words
- Write one scene and a summary of the other scenes in *The Reward* stage of the journey
- Write a summary of all of the scenes in *The Reward* stage of the journey

2) Create a profile for your trickster in 300 or fewer words. Emphasize, not the details of his appearance, but the answers to the above questions in our section on the trickster. What is his specific role in your *Hero's Journey*? How does he offer the hero a different perspective, turning the situation upside down so that the hero can see it differently? Does he bring comic relief, and if so, how? Is the trickster an outlaw and how do you plan to develop that?

3) Write a 500-word scene of action for your hero that includes both tension and suspense. Try to tighten the tension and accelerate the suspense as the scene moves forward. If you're writing a plot-driven story, the tension and suspense will be mostly external, if a character-driven story, mostly internal. And don't forget to include a surprise.

LESSON TEN

THE ROAD BACK, THE ROLE OF THE ALLIES, & INTEGRATING BACK STORY/FLASHBACKS

THE HERO IN STEPHEN KING'S NOVEL, *MISERY*, Paul Sheldon, thinks he's finally rid of the demented woman, Annie Wilkes, who held him hostage and made him write every day, tormenting and torturing him when his writing was not up to snuff—her snuff—only to come face to face at the end of the novel with another woman in a restaurant who quite gleefully tells him, "I'm your number one fan!" These are the exact words that Annie Wilkes said to him when she first brought him into her home.

Most of the time, of course, the hero is able to escape the influence of the shadow character and, having learned his lessons and all that, is not often being stalked again at the end of the story. But I haven't talked to anyone who didn't think this was the most clever ending King could have written for *Misery*. We're all still quoting that line—"I'm your number one fan"--so that should tell us something. King gave his hero an unforgettable *Road Back*.

How can you make your story's *Road Back* just as memorable?

THE ROAD BACK

THE PREVIOUS STAGE IS A LESS DRAMATIC ONE, and so now the hero is dramatically tested one last time. He's nearing the end of his journey, so there's plenty to be afraid of again. Will anyone believe what he's just gone through? Is anyone watching him? Are there enemies out there waiting for the opportunity to take their revenge?

The hero has a choice to make here—will he stay in the special world, or will he begin the journey back to the *Ordinary World*, either to his original starting point or to a new location? A true hero has a desire to now live out the lessons he's learned in the special world, to take them back to his tribe in the *Ordinary World* or to somehow learn to use them to adapt to the special world, should he decide to stay.

Some of the drama on *The Road Back* could come from the shadow character who wasn't completely defeated in the *Ordeal*. Or a character connected to the shadow could show up, threatening the hero in some way. Some heroes are forced to leave the special world, are literally chased out of it. In some stories, on *The Road Back*, after everything the hero has endured, it looks like all is lost. Something happens that threatens all of the hard work the hero has put in, everything he's sacrificed to get to this point. In the movie, *Heat*, on *The Road Back*, Neil McCauley (Robert DeNiro) stops at a hotel to commit one final murder which causes Lt. Vincent Hanna (Al Pacino) to catch up with him and gun him down. A costly mistake on *The Road Back*. In this case, at the end of the story, McCauley, an outlaw/anti-hero throughout the story has now become a tragic hero.

What would the *Road Back* look like for an outlaw/hero? He's the protagonist in your story, so remember, you can't kill him off. I need to mention this once again in case you were thinking about it. Way too many novice writers seem to want to do this—kill off their heroes. I'm not sure why. Can a dead hero talk to us from the grave? Can he write down his story so that we can read it? Not that those who die can't teach us lessons. Of course they can. But they have to be alive in order to communicate those lessons. And if they're no longer alive, well, they're dead, and so you'll have to choose a different character to tell the hero's story. Writers do it all the time, tell the story from a minor character's or narrator's point of view.

So, keeping the outlaw alive, where does he go on *The Road Back*? By this time, our outlaw knows that his unconventional views have gotten him into a pack of trouble. Who is he going to be as he heads back home to the *Ordinary World* or to a new world? How is he going to continue to be who he is and get by without getting into trouble once again?

When I'm teaching sci-fi or fantasy writers what to do with the character arc of their protagonist with a special gift, I list their options on *The Road Back*: 1) the hero loses his gift, 2) the hero decides to keep using his gift, knowing he'll always be in trouble because of it, or 3) the hero decides never to use his gift again. It's not so different with the outlaw/ hero; he can conform to the world of conventional wisdom, he can decide to keep being who he is, challenging authority and suffering for it, or he can decide it's not worth it, staying who he is, but living a quiet life. It seems to me that *Easy Rider* outlaw star, Dennis Hopper, chose the first option in later years before he died—becoming more of a conservative than an outlaw. Comedian Bill Maher is an example of the second option, getting kicked off ABC when happening to mention that the terrorists who planned the 911 attacks weren't, after all, cowards at all, as George Bush had called them, that it took a certain amount of physical courage to pull off what they did. Maher never missed a beat, and is still spouting his unconventional views many years later. Examples of the third option would be Assisted Suicide advocate Jack Kevorkian who never changed his views but no longer helped people commit suicide, and JD Salinger, author of *Catcher in the Rye*, who stayed who he was, but never published much again and lived a reclusive life.

It's up to you—what does your hero face on *The Road Back* that will test his courage, that will squeeze him tighter than he was squeezed in the *Ordeal*?

Does your shadow character show up during The Road Back? What happens during his encounter with the hero?

Is there a chase scene on The Road Back? Is it internal or external, and how does your hero navigate it?

What does your hero have to sacrifice to make sure he gets back?

What happens to make it look like all is lost for the hero? (In the Wizard of Oz, Toto sees a cat, runs after it, Dorothy chases Toto, and the balloon goes up without her.)

If an outlaw, what is the hero thinking about on The Road Back? Who is he deciding he's going to be as the story nears its end?

Ally energy:

• encourages and supports

• challenges conventional wisdom

• eagerly helps and assists

• puts another's agenda before his own

• values loyalty and trustworthiness

• sees the best when the worst seems prevalent

• often shows up as an angel, animal or ghost

THE ROLE OF THE ALLIES

Famous Allies:

Han Solo

Ethel Mertz

The scarecrow, tin man, & lion

Robin (Batman)

Ron Weasley (Harry Potter)

EVERY HERO NEEDS A BUDDY, a support character, a sidekick who has his back throughout the journey. This is often, but not always, a character who doesn't have his own agenda for the hero. You may wonder at times if such a person exists. A person without a personal agenda? Let's at least suspend our cynicism for a moment. This is a character who sees the good in the hero and the good in the journey and just wants to be there for the hero. He believes in the hero's goal, believes the hero is capable and has the resources to achieve the goal. He believes in the hero when the hero doesn't believe in himself.

In prison, who are your allies? I have heard numerous times that it's difficult to find allies when you're incarcerated, hard to know who to trust. At the same time, I've heard, especially older convicts, talk about allies they've had for years and years. Who has aligned him or herself with you in your life goals, your dreams, your passions? If you consider yourself an outlaw, who agrees with your plan to resist conventional wisdom, whether it shows up in an act of civil disobedience or a stubborn refusal to take a plea bargain to get yourself off when you know you can't because you have more integrity than that?

According to Chris Vogler, allies are virtues in the psyche of the hero, which is an interesting perspective. So let's say your hero needs courage (and which hero doesn't?) in order to defeat the shadow and his own weaknesses. His ally, who is not easily threatened (or he would be more of a shadow, threshold guardian, or shapeshifter) has the kind of courage our hero needs.

Ally's purpose:

External:

• to provide companionship

• to show up as a sparring partner for the hero

• to provide comic relief

• to be the hero's conscience

• to serve as an errand boy, carries messages, scouts locations

• to reveal important questions about the plot

• to give the hero someone to talk to, confide in

The ally can bring out the worst in your hero because the hero has many unhealed places, many wounds that still drive him. His allies can surface these wounds in the same way the shadow does, only for a different purpose and with a different outcome. The ally doesn't see the hero as a competitor and he doesn't want to destroy him —that's what makes him an ally. And so he will stay in there, saying things, doing things to support and encourage whenever the hero begins to despair or wants to give up on the journey. Maybe the ally has been where the hero is now going and so he has personal experience to back up his support. Or maybe he just sees something in the hero that the hero doesn't see in himself.

The hero doesn't always listen to his allies, of course. Oftentimes, he doesn't even recognize his allies. Part of the transformation in a hero throughout a story is that he starts out seeing his enemies as friends and his friends as enemies, then learns how wrong he is by the end of the story, and that it's just the opposite—his so-called friends want to destroy him and those characters he doesn't respect because they come off weak or seem to misunderstand what he's about are really the best friends he's ever had.

The challenge for you as the writer, if your protagonist and allies are all outlaw/heroes, is to reveal how, even while resisting authority at times, while questioning conventional wisdom, the hero's allies are still about bringing out the best in the hero, that even though they're all resisting and questioning and fighting the status quo, the allies are only about encouraging and supporting; they have the hero's best interest at heart.

Who are your hero's allies, his sidekicks, and what are their specific roles?

How do the hero's allies support him on his journey as well as challenge him to be more than he is?

What are the virtues that the allies possess and that the hero needs to complete his journey?

Does the hero resist his allies, at least in the beginning of the story? How?

How can you show an ally as both outlaw and support person who wants only the best for the hero?

Ally's purpose:

Internal:

• to challenge the hero to be more open and balanced

• to help humanize the hero

• to represent the unexpressed or unused parts of the hero's personality that must be activated in order to succeed on the journey

• to represent powerful internal forces that can assist in a spiritual, emotional, or physical crisis

• to allow for the expression of fear, humor or ignorance that may not be appropriate for the hero

USING FLASHBACKS (MOTIVATION AND EMOTION)

THE FLASHBACK IS A SCENE FROM A CHARACTER'S PAST that you can use to help reveal motivation. The acts, the words, the thought patterns a character has in the present often have their origin in the past. And so, if you want your reader to fully understand and care about your character, it's sometimes important to re-surface these scenes from the past.

Let's say we have an outlaw who is about to rob a bank, not because he's greedy, but because he has lost his job and can't buy Christmas presents for his wife and kids. He feels like a failure. Most of us, if we found ourselves in this situation, wouldn't choose this route—robbing a bank. What makes

"From the dawn of storytelling, heroes have been paired with friendly figures who fight at their sides, advise and warn them, and sometimes challenge them."

~Christopher Vogler

the outlaw choose it? Something in childhood began to form his personality as an outlaw. What was it? It's up to you as the writer to figure this out, then to insert it into the story at just that point where it's needed in order to give the reader compassion for his choices.

I was married to an outlaw for 13 years who was also a Christian fundamentalist. An interesting combination—an outlaw/Christian fundamentalist. He was never able to integrate these two parts of his personality, and the result was a disassociated human being who had no clue who he was. This created some strange behavior patterns. If I were to ever write his story, I would want to know what happened in his childhood that caused him to both rebel against authority and society, and at the same time demand perfection of himself so that he wouldn't piss God off and spend eternity in a hell of his own creation.

Because the outlaw/hero is often difficult for the average reader to understand or empathize with, the flashback can play a more important role than with other kinds of characters. Remember that the flashback is about motivation. You want to help the reader understand why your outlaw/hero is so angry about a certain injustice taking place in society. Or why something disturbs him that doesn't seem to disturb anyone around him. Sometimes, the outlaw/hero is the lone voice crying in the wilderness.

There are many ways to use the flashback in a story. It can be a developed scene, it can be narrative in the hero's mind. It can be dialogue with another character. The goal is to strategically place the background into the story at the most relevant moment in a scene. The hero may be about to do something the reader just wouldn't believe without the flashback. Or maybe he says something in the middle of a piece of dialogue that again would be unbelievable without the flashback. Sometimes, if a certain event in a hero's past is so dramatic and so influential as to largely determine who he is in the present, you might want to have him re-enter the entire scene, including details. You stop and develop the flashback scene right in the middle of the present scene.

Where you place your flashbacks is almost as important as the information you convey in the flashback. You don't want to stop the story when the action is rolling. For example, you don't want your hero to stop and remember an abusive potty training experience right in the middle of a special kiss or a dramatic car chase.

The length of a flashback is also an important component. You don't need to go on for pages and pages about any aspect of the hero's past. The reader cares about the present story and is often just enduring a lot of flashback material we writers think is so crucial to the story. She just wants us to get back to the present. You engaged her in the present story, and that's the one she cares about.

There are exceptions to everything you'll read in this course. Every once in a while the story comes along that is told best in flashback—the entire story--and framed in the present. But this is the exception.

Used skillfully, the flashback can work well to show the depth of our hero's motivation and can greatly influence the way our reader perceives our hero.

ASSIGNMENT:

WRITE A DRAMATIC SCENE OR A NARRATIVE SUMMARY of your hero's *Road Back*. Does the shadow make an appearance? What does your hero have to sacrifice at this stage to prove that he's serious about the change taking place inside of him and to ensure that he really gets back? What happens to make it look like all is lost and he won't get home, after all? If your hero has a strong outlaw archetype, how is he deciding to navigate in the world once he returns?

1) Please choose one of the following options:

• Write a short *Road Back* scene of 1000 or fewer words

• Write one scene and a summary of the other scenes in *The Road Back*

• Write a summary of all of the scenes in *The Road Back* stage of the journey

2) Create a profile for each of your major ally or allies in 500 or fewer words. Emphasize, not the details of their appearance, but the answers to the above questions in our section on the allies. Focus specifically on their role in *The Hero's Journey*. How does the hero resist them and their support in the beginning of the story? How does his perception of them change as the story moves forward? What do the allies possess in the way of virtues that they can impart to the hero so that he can complete his journey?

3) Write a 500-word flashback scene. Show how what happened in this scene began to form the personality of your hero, how he was wounded, how he took a hit, how he was emotionally impacted at the time by what happened. Don't worry about fitting it into the present-moment story. What's important is to consider that one moment in your protagonist's past that began to put him on what would eventually become his *Hero's Journey*.

LESSON ELEVEN

THE RESURRECTION, OTHER ARCHETYPES & WHEN THE HERO'S JOURNEY IS WORKING, WHEN IT'S NOT

I'VE HAD THE WONDERFUL OPPORTUNITY to observe a number of *Resurrections* as many I've met in the men's prison where I volunteer are released back into the community. Yes, I've seen tragic heroes return to prison, clearly not even close to the end of their journeys, or maybe starting new ones, but I've seen many more defeat their shadows in the final moments of their *Hero's Journeys* to resurrect. These men inspire me time and time again.

One of these young men has become like a family member to me. He's been there for me in a way some of my own children have not been able to be. We celebrate holidays together. After recently expressing a fear that some of my real family members may not accept him at a holiday gathering I was planning, I received an email in which one line stood out: *Trust the goodness in us all, my friend; we might surprise you.*

As the hero nears the end of his journey, there is a goodness in the hero that wasn't there before. He has proven to his tribe, and most of all to himself, that he is a changed person, that he'll be contributing to his world from a place inside of himself that's loving and caring and, yes, good. In our *Ordinary Worlds*, we are all in prison in some way. Our *Hero's Journeys* into our special worlds give us the opportunity to break out of prison and live full lives, grateful just to be alive after all that we've endured on the journey back home.

RESURRECTION

Outlaw's purpose:

External:

• to behave in shocking or disruptive ways

• to act out with illegal/ criminal behavior

• to rebel against conventional wisdom

• to be outrageous

• to attain radical freedom

• to assist in bringing down an oppressive establishment

• to help open and ease social restrictions

• to serve as a safety valve, allowing others to let off steam

THIS STAGE IS THE "CLIMAX" OF THE STORY where the reader watches the hero come up to death one last time, purging the effects of *The Ordeal*—shaking off the toxins while sustaining the wisdom—and coming into his authentic self which, by the way, if our hero is an outlaw, would include the light side of what has appeared up until this point as darkness. The transformation of his soul must tangibly exhibit itself at this point. Just as he became a different person to enter the special world, now he must show how he has integrated the lessons from the special world so that he can re-enter the *Ordinary World*. He is sobered from the battles he's been through and yet lighter for having shed a part of himself he no longer needs.

The most important thing to remember as the hero goes into this final battle is that he must be the one to deliver the death blow to the shadow. While others can step in to help, the final battle is his alone, and he's the one who must save himself. The shadow is, of course, the antagonist, but it's also the dark part of the outlaw/hero that got him into trouble in the first place.

Since *The Resurrection* provides the opportunity for the hero to pass his final exam, the scope of the exam is on a much larger scale. Whereas, his battles, even *The Ordeal*, in the special world was a threat against him and/or his family, now the threat is more universal, against the world. The hero has choices at this point—will he resort to his old ways as he battles this last threat, or will he exhibit that he's a new person with new ways of being in the world? The outlaw challenges conventional wisdom at this part of the story in a redemptive way—his motive is no longer self-serving, but it's for the greater good of the larger community.

The Resurrection may be a dramatic and explosive moment or it might be a quiet moment of epiphany. The hero may experience the climax mentally, physically, and emotionally. He may stumble and drop the ball at the last moment before he crosses back over to the *Ordinary World* which could create a lot of tension for the reader. A false hero could show up to question the hero's credibility or insist that he, rather than the hero, accomplished the impossible and deserves the acclamations the hero is getting. The hero must come up with physical proof that he's who he says he is. This isn't about receiving due credit, it's about honoring his *Hero's Journey;* his transformation is real because of what he has accomplished. He may have to make a final sacrifice. Chris Vogler writes in *The Writer's Journey*: "They [heroes] don't really deserve to be loved until they have shown their willingness to sacrifice."

Subplots (the mini-stories within the larger story) are wrapped up here. And ideally, *The Resurrection* should reveal that the hero has absorbed and integrated the best part of the energy of all of the archetypes; the herald, mentor, shadow, threshold guardian, shapeshifter, trickster, and ally. He's coming home to himself.

What does your hero have to let go of in order to re-enter the Ordinary World? How is he a different person, and how will you show his transformation? Specifically, as an outlaw, how will he now express and exhibit the wisdom he's gained along the way in a more, shall we say, civilized manner?

What is the hero's final test at this stage?

What is the hero's one decisive act that shows his seriousness about defeating the shadow and incorporating the lessons of the special world as he moves forward?

Is the story's climax a dramatic one with lots of noise or a quiet one that shows the steadiness of the hero's new self?

How will you set the stage for the catharsis the reader needs at this point of the story?

Does your hero stumble at all as he's resurrecting? How does he find his footing again?

Outlaw's purpose:

Internal:

• to identity as an outsider, disassociating from the values of society in a way that flies in the face of conventional behaviors and morality

• to challenge the brooding that comes with feeling trivialized or inconsequential

• to cultivate deeper, truer values than the prevailing ones

• to hold the shadowy qualities of the culture—the ones society disdains and disregards

• to express contempt for society's rules

• to justify illegal or unethical strategies to get needs met when healthy and socially acceptable means don't work

• to find a sacred path through revenge to justice to forgiveness

What kind of proof does the hero bring back that he's been on the journey?

What does your hero sacrifice?

OTHER ARCHETYPES

Outlaw energy:

• overturns or destroys what is not working (for the outlaw or for society)

• seeks out revenge

• desires to startle and shock

• reveals the way civilization limits human expression

• pursues goals by unconventional means

• perceives self as powerless, mistreated, under attack

• reinforces soulless, cynical behavior when values are absent

• breaks through dull and repressive thinking

THE PSYCHOLOGIST, CARL JUNG, defined an archetype as a collectively inherited unconscious idea, pattern of thought, or image universally present in individual psyches. So, for example, you may identify strongly with one or more of the archetypes in *The Hero's Journey* as we've studied them in this course. Others not so much. Our archetypes begin to develop during childhood and can become weaker or stronger as we give them a voice or put them away into our shadow.

The conventional list of *Hero's Journey* archetypes as Joseph Campbell put them out there for us includes, as you know by now, the hero, the herald, the mentor, the shapeshifter, the threshold guardian, the trickster, the shadow, and the allies. But a story isn't limited to these eight archetypes, and you, as a writer, aren't limited to them, either. The outlaw, for example, is another archetype that we've been using in this course, with ideas as to how to develop it in your story. In Lesson Two, we listed a few things about this archetype: that his motto is that rules are made to be broken, his core desire is revenge or revolution, his goal is to overturn what isn't working, his greatest fear is to be powerless or ineffectual, his strategy is to disrupt, destroy, or shock, his weakness is crossing over to the dark side/crime, his talent is outrageousness and radical freedom, and that he's also known as the rebel, revolutionary, wild man, misfit and/or iconoclast. Well, there are identifying elements of a large number of other archetypes, as well, that you may want to develop in your *Hero's Journey* story to enrich and broaden its universal truth and deepen its message. There's not room for them all here, but following are some examples to get you started thinking that there might be another one or two archetypes you can use to convey your story's deeper truth and challenge your hero to move forward in yet another way

The explorer is one archetype, not typically identified in a *Hero's Journey* story but who could be a helpful addition to your Cast of Characters: his motto is to resist those who try to fence him in, his core desire is to possess the freedom to find out who he is through exploring the world, his goal is to experience a better, more authentic, more fulfilling life, his biggest fear is getting trapped, conformity, and inner emptiness, his strategy is to seek out and experience new things, to escape from boredom, his weakness is aimless wandering, becoming a misfit, his talent is autonomy, ambition, and being true to his own soul, and he's also known as the seeker, iconoclast, wanderer, individualist, and pilgrim. Similar to the outlaw in some ways which is why I put this forth as another archetype you might want to consider for your story.

There are many more; the king, the priest, the pirate, the networker, the avenger, the lover, the magician, the mystic, the visionary, the servant, the mediator, the engineer, the healer. These are just a few. They all have both light and dark sides, depending on how conscious they are as to their development as human beings and how determined they are to either move toward the light or the dark side. But each of these archetypes has a motto, core desire, goal, fear, strategy, weakness, talent and other archetypes he's known as.

You might want to play around with other archetypes and see if they fit into your story.

Famous Outlaw Heroes

Robin Hood: a folk legend who robbed the rich to give to the poor.

Zorro: a dashing black-clad masked outlaw who went about avenging the helpless, punishing cruel politicians, and bringing aid to the oppressed.

Lucas Jackson: Cool Hand Luke--a prisoner in a Florida prison camp who refuses to submit to the system.

Erik: character in *The Phantom of the Opera*, an "Angel of Music" who extorts money from the Opera's management while teaching the protagonist, Christine, a little bit of heaven's music, enabling her to embark on her career as a successful vocalist in the Opera.

Edmond Dantes: character in *The Count of Monte Cristo*, who, wrongfully imprisoned, escapes from jail, acquires a fortune and sets about getting revenge on those responsible for his imprisonment, but first reaches out to help those who were kind to him before his imprisonment.

HOW TO KNOW WHEN YOUR *HERO'S JOURNEY* STORY IS WORKING

YOU MAY WONDER, IF YOU'RE NEW AT TRYING TO WRITE a *Hero's Journey* story, if you can even trust yourself to know if a scene or a story is working or not. That's fair. When learning to drive, how do you know if you're driving well or not? One indication is if you don't wrap your car around a tree. If you're able to stay in your own lane on the freeway. If you stop at red lights and move ahead on green. Just knowing some of the basics will help you measure how you're doing.

You've taken your hero through the 12 stages, and you've identified your archetype characters which means you now know some storytelling basics which will help you measure your progress as a storyteller. And the more you write, the more you'll begin to understand how to put all of the basics together—when to take your hero through each stage in order and when to take liberty with the stages of your *Hero's Journey*.

Here are some quick guidelines that will help you measure the flow and effectiveness of your story. Your story is working if:

1. You have a hero that is vulnerable and authentic so that the reader will make an emotional investment in your story.

2. You've created a formidable shadow/antagonist who is an even match for your hero.

3. Each stage of the journey takes off, dropping the reader into the action, and your scene and/or chapter endings surprise the reader with a new obstacle for your hero to overcome.

4. Your hero has a conflict in every scene; something is always at stake.

5. Your hero wants something in every scene—he has an external goal and an internal intention and is constantly facing his greatest fear in order to get closer to what he wants.

6. You're resisting the urge to use your hero or other characters to preach, rage against the system, or philosophize endlessly.

7. The setting for your *Hero's Journey* is exotic, fascinating, and/or authentic.

8. You've found your voice for the story.

9. Your hero is able to authenticate and communicate the journey's theme because he's struggled and lived through the truth of it.

10. The reader can't put the story down.

Post these ten guidelines somewhere in your cell or in your writing notebook.

Character arc:

A **character arc** is the status of the character as it unfolds throughout the story, the storyline, or series of episodes. Characters begin the story with a certain viewpoint and, through events in the story, that viewpoint changes. A character arc generally only affects the MAIN CHARACTER in a story, though other characters can go through similar changes. (Wikipedia)

FIXING A *HERO'S JOURNEY* STORY THAT'S NOT WORKING

SO WHAT IF YOU'RE STUCK? You know your story's not working. You can feel it. You may or may not be able to identify the problem. What do you do?

Quit? That's what too many of us do. We put the story away, thinking we'll get it out later and finish it. As if the story will fix itself while it's sitting alone in our writing notebook or tucked away in a box somewhere. We forget about it. We start another story, which we work on until that story stops working. We put it away. And so on. Been there, done that.

One of the reasons we write is to work through personal issues in our own lives, and so when we (if we're writing a personal story) or our hero gets stuck, backed into a corner, and we don't know how to get out, we give up. But it's at those places of getting stuck that the real truth of our story is about to emerge, if we can just hang in there. We have to learn how to write our way through the stuck places.

Following are a few things you can do to get unstuck:

1. Create a new character, and give him an archetype with a new aspect of the truth who can inform the *Hero's Journey* and take it in a different direction.

2. Change the voice: if you're writing in third person, try first, or vice versa; if you're writing a short story, switch to a personal experience story; if the story feels too depressing, try a touch of humor.

3. Put the story away for a set period of time; three days, a week, no longer than a week. Think about it while you're walking, showering, working. Physical activity could jar your stuck thoughts loose.

4. Write some first-person sketches on the archetypes that are getting you stuck. Let them tell you who they are; identify all of their agendas.

5. Put away the chapter or scene you're working on and start a new scene or chapter.

6. Imagine the story from another character's point of view. Is there another way to look at the scene that's tripping you up?

7. Ask yourself what you're afraid to write, what you're avoiding, what you can't face exploring. Drop down a level in your mind.

8. Imagine your reader. What does she want to know? What would she ask your hero right now? What would surprise her?

9. If you haven't outlined your *Hero's Journey* story, consider stopping to do that.

10. Give up the need to control every aspect of your story; at the same time, know that you, not your characters, are the one in control of your story.

If you've tried everything and you still feel stuck, maybe it's simply not the time for you to write this particular *Hero's Journey* story. There's no point in trying to force a story that doesn't want to be forced. Give yourself a break. Know when to put a story away until it calls to you again. And if it never does, let it go. But be sure to try all of the above first, so that you know you've tried everything there is to try.

I hope you're feeling empowered now that you're learning some tools for what it takes to make a *Hero's Journey* story work on the page, for tweaking it if it isn't working so well. You're the storyteller, after all. It's your voice and your truth. You're the one who directs the characters, you're the one who navigates them through the maze to a new place of freedom and transformation.

ASSIGNMENT:

Write a dramatic scene or a narrative summary of your hero's *Resurrection*. What does his final test consist of? Does the *Resurrection* take place quietly or does the hero make a loud statement that reveals his transformation? What does he let go of here at the end, and what kind of final sacrifice does he make that will lead to the *Return of the Elixir* in the final stage of the journey? What is his tangible proof that he's been on a *Hero's Journey*?

1) Please choose one of the following options:

• Write a short *Resurrection* scene of 1000 or fewer words

• Write one scene and a summary of the other scenes in *The Resurrection* stage.

• Write a summary of all of the scenes in *The Resurrection* stage of the journey

2) Create a profile of an archetype not found in a classic *Hero's Journey* in 300 or fewer words. Identify his motto, core desire, goal, fear, strategy, weakness, talent and other archetypes he's known as. How can you use him in the story? What will he add that will enrich your theme? How will he either prevent your hero from moving forward or support him in his quest?

3) Write a 500-word narrative about why you think your story is working—or isn't. Be as specific as you can, identifying the areas that need your attention and the ones you can leave alone.

LESSON TWELVE

RETURN WITH THE ELIXIR, CONNECTING WITH READERS, PURPOSE/MARKETING & THE FINAL CHARGE

I WILL NEVER MAKE THE ASSUMPTION that just because a man is in prison, the dark side of the outlaw archetype has control of him. But the public may make this assumption, whether the prisoner likes it or not. And much, maybe most, of the public knows nothing about *The Hero's Journey*. When they think of the prisoner, they may judge him, not as just having an outlaw archetype, but as a criminal who is most likely not rehabilitated. Nor will he be, released or not. This is simply the reality for outlaws who commit crimes and end up in prison—they are often outcasts judged by society, even once they're released back into society.

The *Return with the Elixir* is proof that the outlaw has been or is being rehabilitated, that he is earning his right to hang out once more with everyone else, that he has learned a few things about keeping the laws of the land. But more than that, he's learned something about himself and how he relates to his world. In its essence, this is what *The Hero's Journey* is really all about—what we learn along the way about who we are as human beings.

RETURN WITH THE ELIXIR

A HERO WHO IS "HOME" FROM HIS JOURNEY is a different person. Even if no one says a word, he knows he's different on the inside, if not on the outside. Metaphorically, the elixir is the internal change in the hero, the lessons he learned on his adventure, the wisdom he now has to share with others.

You may still be wrapping up subplots in this final stage of the journey, and you may want to include a surprise for the hero and the reader. This is your last opportunity to appeal to your reader's emotions; will your ending satisfy or provoke your reader? Some endings circle back around to the beginning, answering all of the questions the hero might have had about himself, his life or the other characters. Other endings are more open, challenging the reader to find her own answers to the questions the hero has lived out in the story.

The reader does want the bad guys to get what's coming to them, and if the ones in your story get off scot free, there had better be a good reason. And this is the exception—not a good idea if you're a new writer because this kind of story has to be handled so delicately. Heroes should also receive their rewards at the end of the story. The elixir is that reward. Think carefully about what you want it to be. At some level, the elixir is what the hero set out to pursue in the *Ordinary World*—it may be something tangible or intangible. According to Vogler, "The best Elixirs are those that bring hero and audience greater awareness."

For the outlaw/hero, it's important to show that, while some of the lessons may have been difficult ones, and the hero had to make sacrifices that hurt him, he is coming home with an elixir that he earned, not because he deserved his reward, but because he walked in all of the integrity that he had. If he continues to challenge conventional wisdom, his challenge comes from a different place than before he became the hero of his journey. His challenge now comes from a place of loving his community and society as a whole as well as himself.

Many new writers rush the ending. Be sure to allow enough room at the end of the story for the reader to say her goodbyes to the characters and absorb the lessons of the story and the recognition of the theme.

The story, just like a sentence, should end with a period, exclamation point, question mark or ellipsis. What does yours end with?

How does your hero prove to those back in his Ordinary World that he's changed?

Does your story conclude with a closed ending or are some things left open? What?

What happens to the shadow and any other characters who have wanted the worst for your hero? Is there poetic justice for them?

What is the elixir for your hero? Is it something tangible or something learned deep inside or both? How does he share it? And if an outlaw, what is the new place our hero comes from that shows up as his elixir?

How can you provide space for the hero's and reader's emotional release? How do you know if you've provided enough space?

How does the Return with the Elixir bring the hero and reader greater awareness?

Does your theme come through clearly?

Have you answered the dramatic question that you asked in the Ordinary World? How does your story end?

THE POWER OF THE *HERO'S JOURNEY* TO CONNECT WITH READERS

I PERSONALLY DON'T BELIEVE THE POWER of either the *Hero's Journey* (many people have never even heard of it) or storytelling itself is given enough credit. We give a lot of credit to the self-help book industry for changing lives, but I have honestly gained more courage and inspiration from reading fictional characters and real people's stories than I have from just about any other medium. It's our sharing our stories with one another that challenges our fears and inspires hope and courage in us to face the difficulties and overcome the obstacles that life throws into our paths.

Just the other day a friend told me that she remembered when the tin man in *The Wizard of Oz* said that, while Dorothy and the scarecrow and the lion all had hearts and so could feel, he had to be careful in his treatment of others because without a heart, he didn't know, couldn't sense when he hurt people. This was meaningful to her in something she was going through in her own life.

In my own life, one paragraph in a novel made a huge difference in a five-year long breech between my youngest son and myself. I quote from my book, *Dialogue* (Writer's Digest Books, 2004):

> It's Emma's words from Larry McMurtry's *Terms of Endearment* to her boys as she lay dying.
>
> "...you're going to remember that you love me," Emma said. "I imagine you'll wish you could tell me that you've changed your mind, but you won't be able to, so I'm telling you now I already know you love me, just so you won't be in doubt about that later."
>
> Emma is an unforgettable character to me because of this one moment where she gives her son, Tommy, the gift of knowing in these words. He's being ornery and his heart is closed to her. He's angry with her for dying. She's going past all of that to let him know that her knowing as a mother

transcends his behavior and closed heart, that she knows deep down in his heart he loves her and while he's forgotten it right now, he'll remember it later.

I've taken Emma's words and have actually used them with my own grown son at this moment in time when he can't reach out, when his heart is closed to me. "I know that you love me," I've told him over and over again. "I know that you love me." It's my gift to him for this time in our relationship.

I heard the actor Sean Penn say one time that if we ever leave a movie theater feeling alone, that movie has failed to connect with its audience. How connected readers feel to our *Hero's Journey* stories is directly determined by how authentically we've created our archetypes, how well they play their roles, and how real we can be when relaying our personal stories. When we're well connected to our own spirits, we can convey our truths to others so as to create a universal connection that causes our readers to feel less alone.

Don't ever underestimate the power of your *Hero's Journey* story to reach into someone's heart and change it forever.

MARKETING YOUR STORY TO THE RIGHT AUDIENCE

JUST ABOUT EVERY SINGLE DAY OF MY YOUNG LIFE I watched my mother who was a successful freelance writer stuff envelopes with her manuscripts, lick the envelopes, and drop them in the mailbox. I was always hopping out of the car and dropping her manuscripts in the mailbox for her. When I started writing myself, I started stuffing envelopes with my manuscripts, licking the envelopes, and dropping them in the mailbox. That's what writers do, don't they? It never occurred to me to do anything different. You write your stories, you stuff envelopes with them, you drop them in the mailbox. (That was during the seventies, of course—now I more often just hit Send on my computer.) It's Writing and Publishing 101.

As a writer with many writing friends and as a writing coach working with many writers, I have found that that's not true at all. More writers don't follow the above procedure than do. Some writers just write for themselves. Some are too scared to send out their work, so they revise forever. Some don't know how to go about it, and so they kind of fumble around forever. Few follow through and persist, eventually publishing their work.

What you do with the *Hero's Journey* story you've worked on in this course is entirely up to you. But you will *do* something. You may put it away, telling yourself it needs work. You may start another story, telling yourself that this one was just an "experiment." You may finish this one and begin the arduous process of looking for an agent and/or editor.

What will you *do*?

Once you've finished writing your story, if you're writing it for someone besides yourself, your next task is to find your audience. Who is going to read your story? If you've written a short story or a short personal experience story, you're looking at magazines. If you're writing a novel or a memoir, of course, you're looking at publishers.

I have always used *Writer's Market* (published by *Writer's Digest Books*) for all of my marketing needs. If the prison librarian is in tune with the needs of incarcerated prisoners, you may just find one in your library. If you know of specific magazines or book publishers you'd like to approach, you can look up their writers guidelines to see if your short story or book length manuscript fits with what they publish.

No matter what you're writing, at some point you'll have to write either a cover or query letter to pitch your story to a book or magazine editor. (A fictional short story is the only kind of story that doesn't require some kind of query to introduce it to an editor; the editor needs to be able to read the entire story because the voice is so much a part of what makes a short story work or not.) But you should still include a cover letter, which is simply a brief form of a query letter.

The first paragraph of your query letter can either be an actual excerpt from the story that presents the hero, the shadow, the setting and hints at the theme and plot all in one paragraph *or* a pitch about your plot or storyline. The idea is to grab the reader with a concise and clear summary about your characters and the situation you've created for them. If the opening paragraph is an excerpt, then summarize the plot in the second paragraph. At the end of this paragraph or in a short paragraph that follows, clearly state your story's theme—what you believe your story to be *about*.

In the next paragraph, you want to introduce yourself. If you have any writing credits at all, mention them. If not, don't draw attention to this by saying something like, "This is my first writing attempt," or "I'm an unpublished writer." I don't have solid advice for you regarding whether or not to mention that you're in prison, but your return address will reveal that, anyway. I would say, definitely mention it if your story is related to your prison experience in any way.

You might want to include a paragraph that states why you think the magazine or publisher is a good fit for the kind of story you've written. You want the editor to know you've done some research, that you've chosen his magazine or publishing house for a reason. Be sure to enclose a self—addressed stamped envelope for the editor's reply.

FINAL CHARGE FOR THE CONFIRMED *HERO'S JOURNEY* STORYTELLER

CHRIS VOGLER (*THE WRITER'S JOURNEY*) WAS ONCE one of the first readers at Disney Studios and rejected 90% of all of the movie scripts that came across his desk because they didn't incorporate some form of *The Hero's Journey*. But even if an editor isn't familiar with *The Hero's Journey*, the elements, stages and archetypes are a subliminal part of the *human* journey and so, he or she will sense if anything is missing, if your story falls apart at any point.

It's true that choosing to use *The Hero's Journey* as a system of storytelling means working hard to make sure that your story connects with your reader in every scene and at every stage of the plot. After all of this, you may decide to just go back to fumbling and stumbling your way along, doing the best you can and hoping your story has enough tense and suspenseful and dramatic elements to keep your reader engaged.

I remember once, after hearing about just how much work goes into telling an effective story, a student in one of my writing classes looked at me with the most serious look on her face, shook her head, and said, "Is there any other way--"

I knew exactly what she was thinking because I hear this question all of the time when teaching both my fiction and nonfiction classes. I interrupted her before she could finish her sentence. "Yes, there is another way," I said. "If you really don't want to have to work so hard at this business of telling stories, there's definitely another way."

She waited for the good news.

"You can decide to be a mediocre writer," I said.

It's your choice. I hope you decide that *The Hero's Journey*, as a system of storytelling, is worth your ongoing effort as far as learning the stages and archetypes and finding a way to use them for the stories you want to tell. For me, *The Hero's Journey* is a system that keeps the storyteller conscious— of developing the characters and moving the plot forward, of engaging the reader at each stage which should be more dramatic than the one before, of the need to present a protagonist who is both fallible and heroic and who inspires the reader to go on and stay on her own *Hero's Journey.*

Yes, writing good stories is work. But it's the most rewarding work you can ever imagine doing. It's the kind of work that entertains while changing readers' lives and causing them to think about themselves in new and challenging ways, which in turn, is the ultimate in satisfaction and fulfillment for you and your *Hero's Journey* story.

Finally, learning to use the *Hero's Journey* to tell your stories is the elixir that proves to everyone out here in society that, as an outlaw, you are not a tragic hero, that you are integrating your prison experience into your being by becoming the hero of your own life.

ASSIGNMENT:

WRITE A DRAMATIC SCENE OR A NARRATIVE SUMMARY of your hero's *Return with the Elixir*. What is the elixir for your hero? Have you fully answered the *dramatic question*, revealing your story's theme? What is the greater awareness for your reader and hero at the end of your story? If an outlaw, how will the hero be a different person, going forward?

1) Please choose one of the following options:

- Write a short *Return with the Elixir* scene of 1000 or fewer words

- Write one scene and a summary of the other scenes in the *Return with the Elixir* stage

- Write a summary of all of the scenes in the *Return with the Elixir*

2) Write a 500-word narrative about your plans for your *Hero's Journey* story now that it's complete. Include a statement about how you want your story to connect with readers.

3) Answer the following five questions; a brief paragraph for each question should be sufficient:

- What have you discovered about yourself as a storyteller/ human being during *The Outlaw's Journey* correspondence course?

- Is writing a story based on *The Hero's Journey* what you expected it to be or did you receive any surprises? Do you think you'll use this system again for other stories you'll write in the future?

- During this course, what did you discover are your greatest writing strengths? What are your writing weaknesses? How can you turn your weaknesses into strengths?

- Which of the scenes/stages that you wrote during the course did you have the most difficulty with? Which one are you the most proud of?

- Overall, how are you feeling about the progress you made on your story during the course?

CONCLUSION

WE HOPE THAT YOU'VE ENJOYED at least the beginning of seeing your or your character's life as a *Hero's Journey*, and that you'll continue to write your stories with *The Hero's Journey* in mind. By this time, we hope you'll agree that both the archetypes and the stages of the journey are powerful tools in the storytelling process as they help writers understand what motivates story characters and how stories move forward, increasing in their ability to challenge the main character to rise to his most authentic and courageous self, whether he's fighting a dragon or conquering alcohol.

We're proud of you for finishing, proud of you for looking deeply into yourself and/or your hero-character to see what makes his particular journey worth the suffering and risk and sacrifice.

Now that you've completed the course, we will be sending you a *Certificate of Completion* sometime within the next two weeks. You can include this in the portfolio you're building to show the DOC, the parole board, whomever's concerned that you're working on yourself, doing all that you can to understand your own drives and motivations, your own human journey.

Congratulations!

APPENDIX I:

WHAT ARE THESE HEROES' FATAL FLAWS?

Jonah (book of Jonah in the Bible) -- Prejudice and bigotry

Jonah wants to believe that God was the exclusive property of Israel. He and his countrymen refuse to allow that God's grace is universal, especially when it means that He extends this grace to the Assyrian city of Nineveh—a cruel and heartless people who skin and bury their enemies alive, or impale them on sharp poles under the hot sun. Politically, Israel (Jonah) is inclusive, trying to form alliances with other nations to ward off any attack from a larger nation, namely Assyria. Religiously, Israel is exclusive, believing that God really doesn't care about other nations besides Israel which prompts the people to be very antagonistic toward other nations. (Sounds a little like today's Christian right.)

Willy Loman (Death of a Salesman) — Self-absorption with personal dreams and desires

Willy has a fundamental flaw in his thinking. He is so preoccupied with his own dreams and desires that he resists and ignores anything contrary to his beliefs. Willy believes that the measure of a man's success is determined by how much wealth he has accumulated and that this wealth is gained by being well liked which eventually leads to his fall. Willy, a tragic hero, recognizes his fatal flaw and decides to commit suicide by deliberately getting into an auto accident.

Voldemort (Harry Potter series) – Exalted sense of self and the need for power over others

He's the smartest and most powerful wizard in the world and he knows it, so he goes out of his way to add a flair of grandeur and grace to his plans while at the same time going about achieving his objectives in as terrifying a way as possible. For example, to amuse himself, he challenges Harry to a duel in the graveyard, when the most pragmatic option would be to simply give the *Avada Kedavra* right there and then when Harry is tied up and can't escape. He doesn't realize that other people could learn about his Horcruxes, or find them, and he certainly doesn't realize that attempting to kill the boy destined to defeat you may result in that boy being actually able to defeat you. And so, Harry Potter is given the weapons to destroy Voldemort.

Harry Potter (Harry Potter series)-- a need to save the world and a martyr complex
Harry is willing to do anything in order to save the people he cares about, but his martyr complex keeps him from asking for help or back-up at times when it would really be a smart idea. He does this to keep the people around him safe, but it tends to work against him.

Heathcliff (Wuthering Heights) – Unforgiveness and Vengeance
Heathcliff holds grudges and spends his life getting even with people who were mean to him. He uses his own family as pawns and holds Kathy on such a high pedestal that he refuses to see that everything that happens to him is not her fault.

John Proctor (The Crucible) – Lust, pride, and deceit

Proctor is an honest and upright man, but his lust for Abigail Williams leads to an affair. Abigail becomes insanely jealous of Proctor's wife, Elizabeth, which sets the entire witch hysteria in motion. Once the trials begin, Proctor realizes that he can stop Abigail's rampage through Salem if he confesses to his adultery. Proctor is a proud man who places great emphasis on his reputation, and a confession would mar that good reputation. He eventually tries to name Abigail as a fraud without revealing the crucial information. When this fails, he finally bursts out with a confession, calling Abigail a "whore" and proclaiming his guilt publicly. This leads to his arrest and conviction as a witch, and though he strikes out at the court and its proceedings, he is also conscious the role he played in allowing this fervor to grow unchecked.

APPENDIX II:

LITERARY MENTORS

SINCE *THE HERO'S JOURNEY* and its archetypes are often accused of being a formula, let's take a creative approach to some examples of the mentor archetype. The mentors below are outlaws, dark mentors, anti-heroes, and traditional wise old men and women. It's no accident that eight out of the nine examples are men; it's challenging to find strong female mentors in either movies or literature, an avenue you might want to explore if you want to do something a little creative in your story.

Meyer Wolfsheim

In F. Scott Fitzgerald's *The Great Gatsby*, Meyer Wolfsheim is a "small, flatnosed Jew" who helps Jay Gatsby make money in the bond business when he first comes to New York after he returns from the war. Wolfsheim seemed to have a dark past; he supposedly was the one who fixed the World Series of 1919.

Mike Cassidy

As a teenager, Butch Cassidy becomes friends with a rustler named Mike Cassidy who teaches him how to shoot. Butch becomes so attached to Cassidy that he takes his last name. Butch loves the outlaw life and follows his mentor out of Utah and into Colorado in 1884 where he begins to get into all kinds of trouble from rustling to train and bank robberies.

William Quantrill

William Quantrill is Frank and Jesse James' mentor; he's the one who teaches them how to kill. He eventually dies from wounds he receives in a skirmish with Union soldiers in Kentucky.

Dumbledore

J.K. Rowling said that her character, Dumbledore, "knows pretty much everything" about the Harry Potter universe: "Dumbledore regrets 'that he has always had to be the one who knew, and who had the burden of knowing. And he would rather not know.'" As a mentor to the central character, Harry Potter, Dumbledore is a wise man who understands that Harry will have to learn a few hard lessons in preparation for what's ahead in his life. He allows Harry to get into the right kind of trouble that he would never allow another pupil to, and he also permits Harry to confront things he'd rather protect him from.

Lestat

Anti-hero and protagonist, Lestat, is the mentor to Louis; he trains and mentors Louis in the ways of the vampire--unusual to him since he had been a human for most of his life.

Brooks Hatlen

In *The Shawshank Redemption*, Brooks Hatlen is a dark mentor for Red, who when he is released from prison, stays in the same boarding house as Brooks, the same bedroom as Brooks, even the same job as Brooks. And Brooks' path leads toward suicide.

The Oracle

The Oracle is Neo's mentor in *The Matrix*. She is the kindly grandmother (like Grandma Moses in *The Stand*) in addition to being the guide. The Oracle provides Neo with key information that is impossible for him to find elsewhere. Though it's dangerous, he seeks her out, not only to gain the information but also because he values her view of him and the path he's chosen.

Gandalf

Gandalf mentors both Bilbo Baggins (in *The Hobbit*) and Bilbo's nephew Frodo (in *The Lord of the Rings* trilogy). As an old, wise wizard, Gandalf researches esoteric lore and provides information about the One Ring and other issues. Gandalf also does his best to ensure that the Hobbits travel with companions whose skills may protect and benefit the quests.

Mr. Antolini

The Catcher in the Rye's Holden Caulfield's mentor is Mr. Antolini, his former English teacher. It doesn't seem to bother him when Holden shows up one time at his house in the middle of the night. During this time together, they discuss Holden's studies at Pencey Perp. Holden vents about how he hated Oral Communication class because whenever someone got up to speak, the other students would yell "digression" whenever the speaker got off topic. Holden admits that he didn't like this at all (not surprisingly, since he is no stranger to digressions himself). Mr. Antolini tells him that the mark of an immature man is that he wants to die nobly for a cause, while the mark of a mature man is he wants to live humbly for one, that among other things, he would learn that he wasn't the first person who was ever confused and frightened and even sickened by human behavior, that he wasn't alone on that score, that many men were just as troubled morally and spiritually as he was at that moment. This is the wisdom of a mentor, one who has gone before.

APPENDIX III:

TEN TIPS FOR CONFRONTING AND OVERCOMING WRITER'S BLOCK

1. Take a moment to consider where you were in the story when you lost your passion. What was going on? Where did you lose the thread? Was it that you didn't know something, and so you felt stupid? Was it that you realized you didn't know where you were going with the story, that you lost sight of your hero's quest? Did something come up in the story you hadn't anticipated?

2. Write daily whether you feel like it or not, and end each of your writing sessions in the middle of a thought or sentence. Sit still for 15 minutes planning where you're going to take your next scene. Your muse will now have something to play with until you're able to sit down again.

3. If you can identify what your sticking point is, come up with a pertinent question that your hero might ask an ally and go around the prison, asking a few guys to answer the question for you; i.e. maybe your mentor is telling your hero something that he thinks is a bunch of B.S.—ask your buds what they would think if someone said the same thing to them.

4. When a true outlaw is stuck, what does he do? He questions, challenges, confronts, argues, makes a general fuss. Put your character in a room with a captive listener and let him expound on the subject that's sticking you in your story.

5. Put the story away for three days. No longer. You don't want to get too far away from it, just far enough to get some perspective. While you're away from your story, write other things—letters, poems, essays, make notes. You can muse on your story, but you can't write on it.

6. Take a walk. Go to the gym. Do some push-ups. When I'm stuck, I often go for a walk and work out the problem with my story while I'm walking. A walk around the yard may clear out the cobwebs from the area of the story that's stumping you when you're just sitting there going over the same stale ideas.

7. Create a new character for comic relief (a trickster) or to confront your hero in a way he hasn't been confronted before. Write this character into a scene with your hero right at the place where you're stuck.

8. Leave off where you got stuck and work on another part of the story. Sometimes it's just that one part that's sticking you, and you can get free if you simply start writing another scene.

9. If your hero or another character is resisting, stubbornly refusing to budge from where he is, you may need to change your perception of him. Maybe he's capable of more than you give him credit for, or maybe he's not as smart, after all, as you need him to be. Let the character lead you. Let him tell you who he is.

10. Be brave and inquire into what the fear is that stopped the flow of your voice. Is it that the guards will show up to do an unexpected strip search of your cell, that they'll snatch your writing, and you'll never see it again? Is it that you know you're not getting out any time soon, and you sometimes really just figure, "What's the point?" Is it that you wonder if you're just writing a bunch of drivel? Well, join the club of Neurotic Artists. These torturous thoughts are just that—thoughts. Now, give them a nod, and get back to work.

APPENDIX IV:

WRITING AND PUBLISHING RESOURCES

NOVEL WRITING

Maass, Donald. *Writing the Breakout Novel*, Cincinnati, OH: Writer's Digest Books, 2002

Vogler, Christopher. *The Writer's Journey*, Studio City CA: Michael Wiese Productions: 2007

Bickham, Jack. *Scene & Structure*, Cincinnati, OH: Writer's Digest Books, 1999

Marshall, Evan. *The Marshall Plan for Novel Writing*, Cincinnati, OH: Writers Digest Books, 2001

Brooks, Larry. *Story Engineering*, Cincinnati, OH: Writers Digest Books, 2011

MEMOIR WRITING

Zinsser, William (editor). *Inventing the Truth: The Art and Craft of Memoir*, Boston, MA: Mariner Books, 1998

Goldberg, Natalie. *Old Friend From Far Away: the Practice of Writing Memoir*, New York: Free Press, 2009

Roorbach, Bill. *Writing Life Stories: How to Make Memories Into Memoirs, Ideas into Essays, and Life into Literature*, Cincinnati, OH: Writer's Digest Books, 2008

Barrington, Judith. *Writing the Memoir: From Truth to Art*, Minneapolis, MN: The Eighth Mountain Press, 2002

Gerard, Phillip (Editor). *Writing Creative Nonfiction*, Victoria, BC, Canada: Story Press, 2001

MARKETING

Burt-Thomas, Wendy. *The Writer's Digest Guide to Query Letters*, Cincinnati, OH: Writer's Digest Books, 2009

Sambuchino, Chuck. *Formatting & Submitting your Manuscript*, Cincinnati, OH: Writer's Digest Books, 2009

Sedge, Michael. *Marketing Strategies for Writers*, New York: Allworth Press, 1999.

Levinson, Jay Conrad. *Guerrilla Marketing for Writers*, Cincinnati, OH: Writer's Digest Books, 2000

Brewer, Robert Lee. *Writer's Market*, Cincinnati, OH: Writer's Digest Books, published annually

BIBLIOGRAPHY

INTRODUCTION

"Wikipedia Contributors." Hero. *Wikipedia*. 17 May 2012. Wikipedia, the Free Encyclopedia. Retrieved 30 May 2012 *http://en.wikipedia.org/w/index.php?title=Hero&oldid=492945135*

Vogler, Christopher. *The Writer's Journey*. Studio City, CA: Michael Wiese Productions, 2007, pages xiii – xiv

"Wikipedia Contributors." The Hero with a Thousand Faces. *Wikipedia*. 1 May 2012. Wikipedia, the Free Encyclopedia. Retrieved 30 May 2012 *http://en.wikipedia.org/w/index.php?title=The_Hero_with_a_Thousand_Faces&oldid=490195586*

"Wikipedia Contributors." Archetype. *Wikipedia*. 15 May 2012. Wikipedia, the Free Encyclopedia. Retrieved 30 May 2012 *http://en.wikipedia.org/w/index.php?title=Archetype&oldid=492697900*

LESSON ONE

"Vogler, Christopher." *The Writer's Journey*. Studio City, CA: Michael Wiese Productions, 2007, page 37

LESSON THREE

"Vogler, Christopher." *The Writer's Journey.* Studio City, CA: Michael Wiese Productions, 2007, page 29

LESSON FOUR

"Frank, Thaisa & Wall, Dorothy." *Finding Your Writer's Voice.* New York, NY: St. Martin's Press, 1994, page 133

"Vogler, Christopher." *The Writer's Journey.* Studio City, CA: Michael Wiese Productions, 2007, page 56

LESSON SIX

"Koontz, Dean." *How to Write Best Selling Fiction.* Cincinnati, OH: Writer's Digest Books, 1981, page 191

"Vogler, Christopher." *The Writer's Journey.* Studio City, CA: Michael Wiese Productions, 2007, page 49

LESSON SEVEN

"Vogler, Christopher." *The Writer's Journey.* Studio City, CA: Michael Wiese Productions, 2007, page 65

LESSON EIGHT

The Outlaw. *Active Imagination.* 2009. Retrieved 30 May 2012 *http://www.marketingforsports.com/content161.html*

"King, Stephen." *On Writing.* New York, NY: Scribner, 2000, Page 201

LESSON NINE

"Petit, Philippe." *To Reach the Clouds.* New York, NY: North Point Press , 2002, page 218

LESSON TEN

"Vogler, Christopher." *The Writer's Journey.* Studio City, CA: Michael Wiese Productions, 2007, page 71

LESSON ELEVEN

"Vogler, Christopher." *The Writer's Journey.* Studio City, CA: Michael Wiese Productions, 2007, page 177

"Wikipedia Contributors." Character arc. *Wikipedia.* 11 April 2012. Wikipedia, the Free Encyclopedia. Retrieved 30 May 2012 *http:// en.wikipedia.org/wiki/Character_arc*

LESSON TWELVE

"Vogler, Christopher." *The Writer's Journey.* Studio City, CA: Michael Wiese Productions, 2007, page 221

ABOUT THE AUTHOR

GLORIA KEMPTON is an author, writing coach and former magazine and book editor. She has written hundreds of magazine articles and short stories, and authored ten books. Her latest book, *Write Great Fiction: Dialogue* was released in 2004 with *Writer's Digest Books*. In the past, she has worked as a freelance book editor for ten major publishers. She's a former Contributing Editor to *Writer's Digest* magazine and has conducted workshops at writers conferences across the country including the Whidbey Island Writer's Conference, the Pacific Northwest Writer's Conference, and the Maui Writer's Conference. She is presently an online instructor with Writer's Digest University *www.writersonlineworkshops.com*, Writers On the Net *www. writers.com*, and Writer's College *www.writerscollege.com*, as well as facilitating online novel and memoir classes of her own. She coaches writers one-on-one in the Seattle area and teaches writing at the Washington State Reformatory. You can contact her at *outlawsjourney@gmail.com*.

EVALUATE *THE OUTLAW'S JOURNEY*

If you don't have enough room, use the back of this sheet. Please return with your last assignment. Thank you so much!

1. What was your favorite part of *The Outlaw's Journey* course?

2. What was your least favorite part of the course?

3. How would you evaluate your instructor's teaching style and feedback on your work?

4. Would you share a few ideas you have for improving our *Outlaw's Journey* course?

5. Would you recommend this course to others at your institution? Why or why not?

Your name (optional)

_____

· Notes ·

· Notes ·

· Notes ·